I0436276

Editor-in-Chief and Founder:
 Lyndon H. LaRouche, Jr.
Editorial Board: *Lyndon H. LaRouche, Jr. , Helga Zepp-LaRouche, Robert Ingraham, Tony Papert, Gerald Rose, Dennis Small, Jeffrey Steinberg, William Wertz*
Co-Editors: *Robert Ingraham, Tony Papert*
Managing Editor: *Nancy Spannaus*
Technology: *Marsha Freeman*
Books: *Katherine Notley*
Ebooks: *Richard Burden*
Graphics: *Alan Yue*
Photos: *Stuart Lewis*
Circulation Manager: *Stanley Ezrol*

INTELLIGENCE DIRECTORS
Counterintelligence: *Jeffrey Steinberg, Michele Steinberg*
Economics: *John Hoefle, Marcia Merry Baker, Paul Gallagher*
History: *Anton Chaitkin*
Ibero-America: *Dennis Small*
Russia and Eastern Europe: *Rachel Douglas*
United States: *Debra Freeman*

INTERNATIONAL BUREAUS
Bogotá: *Miriam Redondo*
Berlin: *Rainer Apel*
Copenhagen: *Tom Gillesberg*
Houston: *Harley Schlanger*
Lima: *Sara Madueño*
Melbourne: *Robert Barwick*
Mexico City: *Gerardo Castilleja Chávez*
New Delhi: *Ramtanu Maitra*
Paris: *Christine Bierre*
Stockholm: *Ulf Sandmark*
United Nations, N.Y.C.: *Leni Rubinstein*
Washington, D.C.: *William Jones*
Wiesbaden: *Göran Haglund*

ON THE WEB
e-mail: eirns@larouchepub.com
www.larouchepub.com
www.executiveintelligencereview.com
www.larouchepub.com/eiw
Webmaster: *John Sigerson*
Assistant Webmaster: *George Hollis*
Editor, Arabic-language edition: *Hussein Askary*

EIR (ISSN 0273-6314) *is published weekly (50 issues), by EIR News Service, Inc., P.O. Box 17390, Washington, D.C. 20041-0390. (703) 777-9451*

European Headquarters: E.I.R. GmbH, Postfach Bahnstrasse 9a, D-65205, Wiesbaden, Germany Tel: 49-611-73650
Homepage: http://www.eirna.com
e-mail: eirna@eirna.com
Director: Georg Neudecker

Montreal, Canada: 514-461-1557

Denmark: EIR - Danmark, Sankt Knuds Vej 11, basement left, DK-1903 Frederiksberg, Denmark. Tel.: +45 35 43 60 40, Fax: +45 35 43 87 57. e-mail: eirdk@hotmail.com.

Mexico City: EIR, Sor Juana Inés de la Cruz 242-2 Col. Agricultura C.P. 11360 Delegación M. Hidalgo, México D.F. Tel. (5525) 5318-2301
eirmexico@gmail.com

Canada Post Publication Sales Agreement #40683579

Postmaster: Send all address changes to *EIR*, P.O. Box 17390, Washington, D.C. 20041-0390.

Signed articles in *EIR* represent the views of the authors, and not necessarily those of the Editorial Board.

One Minute To Midnight

It's Time To Denounce the Saudi Barbarism and Bankrupt Wall Street

Jan. 3—Justice for the victims of the Sept. 11, 2001 attacks has been obstructed for too long by George W. Bush and Barack Obama; and now, heading off a world war depends on that justice being rendered.

The mass executions by the barbaric Saudi regime on Jan. 2, which are now polarizing the entire Muslim world again, must be denounced widely by all civilized people, before Saudi actions trigger a new global war.

The first and immediate step must be the immediate release of the secret 28 pages from the original Congressional Joint Inquiry into 9/11, which detailed the direct role of the Saudi Monarchy in organizing those attacks on New York and Washington. President George W. Bush buried those 28 pages, and President Barack Obama has kept them buried. House bill H.Res. 14 and Senate bill S. 1471 demand their release. But the time has come to bring the contents of those 28 pages to the floor of the House and Senate, and to all Americans.

Had those contents been out, there would be no Islamic State threat today, and the Saudi sponsorship of global jihadist terrorism would have been halted thirteen years ago. The actions by Bush and Obama, in protecting that dirty Saudi secret, are tantamount to acts of treason against the American people, starting with the 3,000 Americans who perished in the Sept. 11, 2001 attacks.

The barbaric mass executions on Jan. 2 should be the clearest reminder that the leadership of the Kingdom is indistinguishable from the leadership of ISIS.

We also stand at one minute to midnight before a financial crash worse, in its effects on people, than 2008.

Today, Jan. 4, begins the policy of "bail-in" all over Europe and in the United States. Government regulators and bankers know the policy; but you probably don't: They will try to "recapitalize" any bank that fails,

by taking its creditors' bonds, and then taking its depositors' money.

And banks will fail. In Europe a string of bank failures and bail-ins of savers has already hit Italy and Portugal just before New Year's Day. In the U.S. financial system, the "junk debt" bubble connected to commodities has gotten 150% larger than the 2008 subprime mortgage bubble ever was; and the delinquent part of that junk debt suddenly spiked in December to 25%—that's as high as subprime mortgage defaults ever got, before the banks crashed.

Clear and direct action is required against Wall Street. The bail-in swindle has been embraced by President Obama and passed into law, in the Dodd-Frank Act, by a cowardly and corrupt U.S. Congress. That Congress reconvenes Tuesday, Jan. 5—its feet must be held to the fire immediately.

Congress could have shut the Wall Street casino down in 2010, by restoring the Glass-Steagall Act and other measures of President Franklin Roosevelt's first months in office. Congress caved in to Wall Street instead. They passed trillions in bailouts and then a Dodd-Frank Act which is now about to produce the even more devastating bail-in—bailing your savings into insolvent banks. Now, the Wall Street/London banking system which is set to blow, can really kill you.

No consideration should be given to any more bailouts, or any bail-ins. Wall Street has no authority to collect these bad debts or replace them with your savings. To prevent economic catastrophe and general war, shut Wall Street and Obama down.

Make them put Glass-Steagall through now! House bill HR 381 and Senate bill S. 1709.

Former Maryland Governor Martin O'Malley has stated the intention to restore Glass-Steagall more clearly than any other Presidential candidate—the *Wall Street Journal* called him "Wall Street's enemy number-one" as a result. Will he get the support to do it?

EIRContents
www.larouchepub.com Volume 43, Number 2, January 8, 2016

Cover This Week

Norwegian Coast by Moonlight, by Andreas Achenbach (1815-1910).

A Force Which Can Resuscitate The United States

Edited excerpts from Lyndon LaRouche's dialogue with the Manhattan Project of Saturday, January 2, 2016

Dennis Speed: My name is Dennis Speed, and on behalf of the LaRouche Political Action Committee, I want to welcome you to our first meeting of the New Year. I think everybody basically knows the procedures. I see a few people who are new here.... So, Lyn, I'd like to give you the opportunity to say something to us, now that we've started a completely new year, and you're with us.

Lyndon LaRouche: Yes. We have to cope with the fact that we are facing a disaster. Now, the disaster has two phases. One phase is the fact that people are struggling to understand something about things, and the second thing is, they find out that it's a disaster. And, so, our question here and our problem here, is to get out of the disaster. And, I think the questions, and discussion matter that has come up in this course, will be of that significance.

We're in a disaster. We, in the United States, as well as in other parts of the world, especially in the trans-Atlantic region, are in a disaster. And, there's very little hope from that, on the basis of the surface, now.

So, this is the challenge. The United States is on the verge of being disintegrated, along with most of the people of the trans-Atlantic area. And our object is to get rid of Obama, and to get a form of Presidential institution, and similar institutions, which are suited to the needs of humanity.

Right now, you have to face the fact, that we are now under a threat of almost extermination. That's what has happened. And, the British Empire has been, of course, the source of this. The trans-Atlantic community is disintegrating, generally. And, the question is, how can we take the situation, in that form, and find a solution?

Asia is strong, but Asia is going to be drawn into a thermonuclear war, unless we can stop the war. And therefore, we have a terrible fate before us, unless we can work our way out of it. And I think we should probably start from my remarks to that effect now, and open the discussion on the same matter from people here

Saint Paul Delivering the Areopagus Sermon in Athens, by Raphael, 1515.

who are reacting.

Speed: Very good. Lyn, I also have a few questions, which I got via Internet, which is a bit unusual. But, I think it's because it's the first of the year, and some people I got out some messages to, late last night, about what the urgency of this situation was, got back to me with a couple of questions. So, I may wish to go to the microphone, myself, at one point, and let you know what those are.

LaRouche: Don't tear your voice apart. It's valuable.

A Deadly Problem for Mankind

Question: Hi Mr. LaRouche. This is R——, from Bergen County, New Jersey. I have a question about executive power. . . . To me, it's pretty clear that over the last 15 years, the Executive branch has grabbed more power than they should have, and the Congress seems to have done very little to check that. How could that situation be corrected? Could it be corrected under the current form of government? And, assuming that there was a more rational form of government in place, how would that have to be corrected?

LaRouche: Well, right now, what we have in Asia— in major parts of Asia, not the entirety of it—but Asia, in general, is a viable institution. Whereas the trans-Atlantic community is not a viable institution. And so therefore, you can take that contrast, and look at the one side, and the other side, and you begin to get what the problem is. What happened is, generally, the British Empire has dominated things since before the beginning of our own Presidency—and, so, since that time, we've had degeneration as a trend in the trans-Atlantic community.

What we have now is a shift in that, in terms of parts of Asia—including Russia, on the edge of it—are really factors, which can play a leading role, for the nation as a whole. But, the trans-Atlantic community is totally corrupt, and has to be changed. So, therefore, what happens is you get President Roosevelt, for example. What happened is, President Roosevelt's intention was destroyed. It was destroyed by the Republican Party, against him. And, what's happened since then: In my life experience, I was thrown in the jug. I was a leading figure in the organization of the Presidency at that time. I was a key vehicle to pass the drama, from what had occurred in that decade, and I passed it on to President Reagan. I was put in prison, because they wanted to get rid of me. And, a lot of people just went the other way, and when I got dumped out, they went back to Satan for succor.

So, that's what the situation is. We have to realize that the United States is ruled by—first of all—is ruled by an evil man, actually a collection of evil men. Bushes—and Bushes that didn't burn, but should. And Obama. And Obama is a Satanic figure. And, most of the people in the United States are intimidated by the presence of this Satanic figure called Obama! And everybody likes to kiss his rear end. I don't, but most of the people in Wall Street do. But they're going to die. Wall Street is going to die! Right now! Because, in the present system, the whole thing is going to collapse. Which means, the whole system of economy, under the present conditions and management, will collapse.

This is a threat of extinction of the citizens of the United States, and other parts of the world. And unless we can come up with a magic instrument by which we can solve this problem, there's not much hope for humanity. Now, this the kind of thing which has happened in past history. It happened repeatedly: Dark Ages. Dark Ages are part of the history in mankind's life.

And, therefore, you have two categories. You have the category which is the humanistic view, which sees progress, which sees goals, and which sees a higher value of mankind. The practical man often tends to be a stupid man. Because he tries to use mechanisms of decision, to decide what is true and what is not. The true man, the real man, is one who's creating a state of mind in the population, a state of mind which was greater, more advanced, richer, more enjoyable, than anything before.

Now there have been periods of ups and downs in the history of mankind, where things sometimes have gone up, and more often have come down. And our concern is don't try to adduce the history as simply a fact, which has occurred by some accident, or some happening. Mankind is right now in deadly danger. The very existence of the human species is in a deadly situation.

On the one hand, you have something in Russia, China, and some other areas,—as opposed to what you have in the trans-Atlantic community. The trans-Atlantic community, and its relationship is a disease, it's a threat to the very existence of the human species throughout the planet. And, our challenge is, we have to take a fighting position, to make sure that we don't go the Obama way, or the Bush way.

Manhattan

And, therefore, we are going to try to get a movement in history, with the aid of Russia, with the aid of China, with the aid of others from that sector, and to use that contact as a stimulus inside the United States, inside Europe. Because Europe is dying. Europe right now is *rotting*. Its rotting out. And, there's no light in sight.

And so, therefore, that's the situation we have. We have a deadly problem for mankind. All mankind is threatened. Now, mankind has been threatened in that way, in that manner, many times in the course of man's general history up to this present time. But, what we're going into now, is a very Dark Age. It's a Dark Age which is characterized by the British culture. And, that's the problem.

So, therefore, what is required of us, is to have the power of imagination, like people who have done that before, in earlier periods of history, of Renaissances and great periods of moment; and our challenge is to bring forth those kinds of solutions. As, say, from the Renaissance period, or what Kepler did, and what Leibniz did, and what we're trying to do, otherwise. These things require us to *search ourselves* to locate those principles and those actions, by which mankind has achieved restoration of humanity, repeatedly. And therefore, we have to become that force. We have to become that influence. We have to give that inspiration, to people who are demoralized by the conditions of life they experience.

This is particularly the case of the trans-Atlantic region. The trans-Atlantic region is now a *disaster*, with very few exceptions. It's going to Hell, with very few opportunities of success. And, that's the problem. We face something, where the imagination of the thinking population,— Now, just one little thing I want to put in on that point: *Manhattan*. If you look now, with the exception of certain spots, local spots inside the United States in particular, there's *nothing*, there's nothing waiting for mankind in general right now, under present conditions.

And therefore, we have to understand this problem, and we can, as we have before, as the Renaissance did, as had been done before the birth of the United States,— these kinds of things have happened. But they don't happen accidentally. They happen by the influence of people, of certain people, groups of people, who save mankind from *Hell*, or Hellish existence. And, we're in such a period, now. And right now, Russia, China, and

other nations of that connection, they are the main means by which we may escape all kinds of Hell, very fast, very soon.

Question: Hi. How are you?
LaRouche: I'm not too bad, for an old geezer.

Question: [follow-up] You look great. This is J— from Brooklyn, and I've been thinking about several questions, or several comments, and I was wondering which one I would bring up today.

Just recently, this past week, a group of us, who are involved in the Manhattan Project, our intention was to go and see Congress people and bring our materials and talk about the urgency of the crisis we are facing and get action, get things rolling, get things done, not just talk any more, but actually demand and challenge them to do something. So, this was Tuesday. We discovered that not only,— well, we went to see one Congress person who did have some people in his office, two people. Then, when we were planning to go to the other places, we discovered that these cowardly, jackass Congress people had shut down their offices. And we called person after person, office after office, and these offices were shut down. I guess they were having New Year's Eve early.

So, that was Tuesday. New Years' Eve wasn't till Thursday, why is there no one in their office; your constituents may actually need you? So, we were kind of discouraged by that. Except for the enthusiasm of one secretary about our music program, after she discussed it with one member.

So, if you could comment on the connection between the music and what we're trying to do to get the people, not just Congress people, but everyone, to understand the urgency of getting Glass-Steagall in place and getting rid of Obama, if you could comment on that connection again, I would really appreciate it.

What Can We Do?

LaRouche: Well, you noted, probably, because you've been watching this process, what we've accomplished,— we had two choruses, together embracing a population of about 1,000 people on Saturday and Sunday. Now, at this point, I would say that Manhattan is now the soul of the United States. Because what you've seen, by these choruses, the formation of these choruses, and to get people to turn out in numbers of 1,000 between the chorus and those that are sitting there

Soprano Rosa D'Imperio during the Schiller Institute's performance of Handel's Messiah on Dec. 20, 2015 at the Unitarian Church of All Souls in Manhattan.

and enjoying the program, this is something absolutely unique since a very long time, and it's unique actually to Brooklyn and Manhattan.

That in general, you can say, with a few exceptions like some localities in the West Coast, and it's with those exceptions,— there's nothing that is not demoralizing about what the people of the United States are experiencing now. And they reflect that. What drives them wild? They have children who are immoral, who are stupid, who are stupefied, who are destroyed,—they're not capable. They are criminal in their proclivities. And this is all over the United States. You have the local cities, and local towns in various parts of the United States. Most of these communities are corrupt. They're rotten in the sense that they have no capability of defining a perspective which humanity would want.

The one area which is most important for the United States *is Manhattan* and the immediate surroundings. That's the chief place of growth in the United States. You have some local spots in California, the middle part, mostly our people. One or two people here or there, something like that. But the general population is demoralized and is *de*-moralized in the literal sense. They've given up.

The young people are degenerate, in general, that is, the characteristic is degenerate; they are not responsive to reality. They don't believe in the truth, and they're little animals, with bad habits. And that's what's been done to them. They didn't do it. But you have a whole generation which, in this process,— and I've seen this,

I've lived through much of this period, and I can tell you the degeneration as I have experienced it directly, throughout the United States and the same thing in Europe. Europe is somewhat a different case, but it's the same principle. What happened in Canada? The mass deaths in Canada just recently? [The rash of economic suicides centered in Alberta.] All of these things show a civilization which is ready to die, or to come close to dying, to extermination of mankind as we know it.

Now there have been periods of evil, for example after the Renaissance, the great Renaissance. The great Renaissance was followed by, actually, a satanic program run by the Catholic Church. Then there was a fight to get that Satanic group out. And Kepler started something in his own way, under conditions of defeat; he died under conditions of defeat. But then with Leibniz, Leibniz's influence drove civilization upward. And so, therefore, we depend upon these kinds of patterns, and so we read these patterns,—like I read the patterns, and say, "we are going into Hell. This is the direction we are going."

We have to fight against going into Hell, which is what we are fighting. We have children, young children, throughout the United States, and they are adolescents and more, and they're degenerate. Look at their music. Look at their behavior. Look at the fruit of their behavior. What you're looking at is the self-destruction of mankind. You're seeing it in the United States; you're seeing it throughout Europe. Europe in general is degenerate. The British system, of course, has been a leading influence in that process.

So the thing we have to look at is the fact that we are facing an age of degeneracy. But there have been periods of degeneracy before,—like the Renaissance, itself, was a freedom from degeneracy. And therefore, our job is to organize mankind to free itself from periods of degeneracy, and the periods of degeneracy have been recurrent, and unfortunately, numerous, in the different parts of the planet.

Then you have also the other types of problems, problems which are sort of practical interpretation problems. For example, Russia under the Soviet system. Stalin was a very loyal person for Russia and for Europe. *But!* he believed that everybody had to behave the way *he* wanted them to behave, and he would actually kill people, leading people, or suppress them, imprison them, because they wanted to manage him. He wanted them to obey him. Now what he demanded of Russians for obedience was not all bad. But the practice that he did, in saying, I'm going to kill people, if you don't do as *I* tell you, which is what his problem was. And so we're in such a period where we have to say, we have to build up throughout the system, the system of mankind, and we have sources in China, sources in India again today, Egypt is a positive factor. And Russia is a very important factor in this thing. And Putin has more or less licked the Stalin problem.

Gottfried Leibniz (1646-1716), who took up Kepler's ideas to advance a new Renaissance.

What We're Up Against

So these are the kinds of things. And therefore, the point is, can we—as individuals and groups of individuals—can we influence the process of redemption of mankind by influence, by good contributions, good ideas, good principles? And we're at a point where we, in Manhattan in particular, Manhattan is the best hope of the United States. Anything outside of Manhattan is not likely to be very important any more. It's true. It's not braggadocio, it's good luck.

We know there are a lot of crooks in Manhattan. They're abundant, and they're mostly Wall Street types. And look at the education system. Look at the education system in California. Do you want your child to be educated by the California school systems and universities anymore? It's degeneracy! And therefore, we have a mission here. Here we are, and what we've had in the two cases just recently, Saturday and Sunday, we had about 1,000 people, both singers and audiences, between the respective places, Brooklyn and Manhattan, and we produced an effect which has not been available to *anyone* in any significant degree heretofore. So therefore, we have an obligation, a moral obligation to convey the essence of what we have accomplished in Manhattan, through the musical expert activities we have been working toward, and that's the *hope* of mankind. And therefore we're going to have to say that we've got something in Manhattan and its associations which is the secret of the successful future of mankind.

Q. Hi Lyn, it's M— from Manhattan. One of the things that I was struck by, actually yesterday, coming home from my temple,— but I'll preface it by this. A friend of mine travels all over the world, that's the job. And this person said, "There's really only one group of people that hate us." "Oh? A group of people hate us? Oh, who could they be?" He said, "They're called Wahhabis." "Wahhabis, what's that?" "Well, that's Saudi Arabia. That's a Wahhabi, and they hate the hell out of Americans." "Oh? Really? Uh-huh." And then coming home from my Buddhist temple yesterday in the car, the driver said, "Oh, yes, well, you're talking about Wahhabis. They own and built every mosque." I said, "Wait a minute. You're going to tell me that these mosques that we have in New York and all over the place were built by the Saudis, who are Wahhabis?" "Yes, you betcha. Yes, they were."

And then I got thinking about what you had mentioned before—the 28 pages, of course—and that these fellows that slit the throats of the airline stewardesses and took all these flying lessons were actually staying with an FBI informant. So there's a connection there to the FBI.

LaRouche: [Laughs] I think a great deal about that. I can tell you that much. No, this is all real. It's fully real. There's been a process from 9/11, and you can go back to the 9/11 events, when these two planes were taken captive in Boston, and were circling around southern Manhattan. I was watching this thing, because I was watching the film of the two planes which had been captured with their passengers. They would come around the towers of lower Manhattan, and crash into the towers. In the process of crashing into the two towers, the two towers collapsed and the people in them and around them died.

It was the Saudis, however, who had set this into motion, under British direction. That's how it happened. This is one of my areas of expertise. I've been working on this, and know that the British Empire and the Saudis, who are stooges for the British Empire, and the Saudi representatives in the U.S. offices, that is, as representatives from Saudi Arabia and Britain,— that the British Empire, the British monarchy, and the Saudis committed this mass murder against the people of the United States, a smaller number at the Pentagon, and many more in the southern part of Manhattan.

And so what conclusions must be drawn from this? Well, then go to the next step. The United States Congress suppressed any action against the Saudi action and the British action, and they have continued that to the present day. So therefore, who's running this? Well, the Bush family was already running it. Obama has been running it.

Frightened People

Obama has been killing people every Tuesday, people who were innocent, who were selected for being murdered by the President, Obama! Now, this is the world we live in. Europe is disintegrating. Western and Central Europe are disintegrating now. How far that will go is uncertain. However the British again are back in the business—the British and the Saudis, and the British and the Saudis are the same thing. The British monarchy and the Saudis are the same thing. Eh? They are mass murderers. And nothing has been done, much, to correct those problems. The victims of 9/11, the Congress! Huh? The government, have all protected this thing, supported it! And we are supposed to subject ourselves to the opinions of the authorities, of people who've done that to us in the United States, who have

Crown copyright (open government license)
Buddies in Satanic crime: British Prime Minister David Cameron and King Salman of Saudi Arabia at the G20 Summit in Turkey in Nov. 2015.

done the similar things throughout various parts of the planet? Where is our President? We don't have a President! We have a piece of filth. Obama. He's rotten! He's evil. He's intrinsically evil, systemically evil. His stepfather was evil.

So these are the kinds of things that we're up against. Now, if you go back into the history of mankind, you find periods in which the Satanic element, which is fairly called the Satanic element, keeps recurring. The great Renaissance—that was suddenly aborted after the end of that particular century, and we went to a period of evil. Kepler, himself, the great Kepler, was under the influence of a great evil that was going on in Europe at that time. Then you got a turn, an upturn. And it happened. Then Leibniz died. Leibniz had been one of the great creators of the Renaissance, the new Renaissance. And when Leibniz died, then, what later became the United States, became a part of the British influence of corruption.

And you look at the number of Presidents we've had, the total Presidents, and you find that most of the Presidents of the United States were really rotten. They were evil people, or stupid, or criminal types of people. And that's the point. And so therefore we have to understand that we have to use our own influence, our own moral standards.

Russia now happens to be a very useful place for us, because of what Putin represents. Russia was not always a good place, but Putin has made it a good place, relatively speaking, and we have other parts of Asia which are on the right side.

At the same time, you have people who are demoralized, but who would also agree that these things which happened were evil; but they say, "I'm scared; I'm scared." Therefore, my particular concern has always been: Where does the evil come from, what is it, and what's the problem that makes people scared so that they aren't able to do something for their own selves, for mankind? All these kinds of things,—what do we do about it? How do we give them the courage?

The Moral Factor

And what I've seen recently, with what I've seen between Saturday and Sunday with the 1,000 total participation, in Manhattan and Brooklyn,—this has changed everything. And Manhattan is the only place in the United States in which a phenomenon like this could've occurred. And therefore my point here is, okay, fine. If Manhattan is going to be the place that re-initiates the United States, well, you have to say, "That's a pretty good idea, it's a pretty good job, considering the job." What's wrong with the rest of the United States, except for a few spotty areas where some people are of a higher grade? The United States is dominated by degenerates! And you have a few people who are the actual heroes, and this has often been the case in history,—that a small part of a population becomes a factor of influence which can bring an evil nation, an evil people, out of their evil into doing creative work. And that has been the history of the United States Presidency. We've had a few great Presidents. We've had many skunks who were Presidents. And therefore you have to take the few who actually represent a leadership factor, a moral factor. You have to bring them together. Assemble them as a force,

Library of Congress

One of the heroic U.S. Presidents, John Quincy Adams (1829-1833). This daguerreotype was done in 1843, when Adams was serving in Congress.

and let their influence go to work.

Question: Hi, Lyn. A— here in New York. M— is a tough act to follow, but I'm going to do my best. In our last discussion on the phone, you responded to what I raised by talking about the failure of our citizenry for a long time always to recognize the principle of Congress, and within your comments you stated that we needed to mobilize the population by itself, in a sense, to whatever we can to contribute to make that happen. Now earlier, a few days ago, I was invited to join a phone call on the Manhattan Project and the operation of developing and aiming at the Bronx, the Borough of the Bronx, to do work and get Glass-Steagall through, through this process.

So this is the choral principle in action, it seems to me, and programs and other things were discussed; I was able to contribute something along the lines of demographics, but the main thing is, this principle of, — well, this idea of what you're saying of organizing the population by itself, and then, what we're doing here, they seem to go hand-in-hand, and yet, I'd really like to hear greater elaboration from you on that.

The Principle of Mankind

LaRouche: Yes, I think it does require that, because it's not as simple as a simple expression would suggest. No, the problem is, when you get people who have a sense,— well, look, everything that's good about mankind is always based on the next generation ahead. That's the principle of mankind. The goodness of mankind comes out of those people who gather, in a sense, to a common sense that the future is needed. For example, take the case of the United States today, in California. Look at what's happening in California, the degeneration, the moral degeneration of the youth in

California, that is destroying the United States, that kind of thing, that pattern.

Now, this came out of the Twentieth Century, because a change came about when Bertrand Russell got involved, and Bertrand Russell's influence, even after he died, has corrupted the United States, as the trans-Atlantic area as well. You actually have a much better perspective for mankind in China; possibly in India, which is struggling to recover itself; and other locations, special locations; and Russia.

So therefore the hope of mankind is located in the composition of these elements, of this region. The general case on the planet, is that the trans-Atlantic area is the area of great danger. The British Empire is evil; the Saudis are evil, I mean, all the Saudis of the Saudi tribes are evil! They are Satanic, literally Satanic! They kill, they kill *en masse*, they kill humans *en masse* throughout Europe and this area! There's no hope for mankind in this area.

Then you find in Germany, Germany took a certain step toward help for people who were abandoned and driven out of the land, and then you had [Finance Minister Wolfgang] Schäuble, this official, who's a *killer*, a stinking killer! And you look at France, well, I don't think there's much in France; there may be some good people in France, but there's not a France which is going to lead Europe in any way into good ends.

So therefore, you're in this kind of situation. And the danger now is, even though China is making a great contribution; India is trying to recover its possibilities, again; Russia is playing a very leading role, on behalf of mankind; while Spain, Portugal, so forth, and so on, are rotting away. And therefore, the problem comes down to, is there a faction, as in the case of what happened in 9/11: is there a faction of forces, which has the capability of devoting itself to freeing mankind of these kinds of evils, of the type I've referred to in general?

And my view has been that. My own devotion has always been in that direction, to provide the kind of leadership which *sees the future*—not the future simply as a phenomenon, but the future as a better condition of mankind, the idea of higher scientific and technological capabilities, the idea of better education; getting people out of the mud. And what we've been living through, since I was thrown in the jug, out of the Reagan Presidency,— I've seen for the main part with a few pieces of exception, a degeneration of the United States as a whole, and of the people of the United States. Why did they degenerate? Because they're social, and when they get into these social influences, it's like the guy who wants to marry seven wives, or something like that; this is a very bad idea; it's also very expensive.

But anyway, the problem is, we're looking for leadership of a kind which can become infectious, which induces people to appreciate the fact that they have access to choices of behavior which are rewarding from the standpoint of mankind. It's like Leibniz in his own time, and people like that. So it's the great leaders in society who often start with limited numbers of people, but who actually make a contribution in an infectious way, to inspire people to discover a better way of living. And without that factor, mankind has very poor chances of survival.

Mobilizing Ourselves

Everything the United States has accomplished, has been despite all the evil people who were President of the United States; most of the Presidents of the United States were evil, in their history! You had a few exceptional people as Presidents. And what we got, we got that way: We got Franklin Roosevelt. Franklin Roosevelt was a real genius in that respect: Here he was, a man who was suffering from a terrible disease, and yet he was able to provide leadership to mankind in the United States, at a time that the United States *had lost* the ability to survive! And then, at a certain point, the FBI took over. And the FBI destroyed that. But we had some people who were responsible people, who fought against this.

But more recently, I was a key figure assigned to the transition to Ronald Reagan. He was not fully functional as a President at that time, and I was one of the two people who was assigned to get Reagan's administration into order. And what happened is, they tried to kill him—by a Bush family member—and I was dumped, and since that time, in general, the Presidency of the United States has been for the most part, with one exception, a bad joke.

And therefore my view is, I have a commitment not to put up with that crap any longer!

Question: Hi, I'm E—N— from Philadelphia, and an activist for the LaRouche organization for years. I give you greetings; we've had the Pope in Philadelphia for Family Day 2015, but overlooked in Philadelphia was the 57 public schools closed down! Forty-plus students in the public school area in each class now. The pressure's put onto these families moving their children around to the schools that are left; nothing has been said about any kind of conditioning of high school students geared for college. And I'm giving you that question now. Mr. LaRouche, what is your ...?

LaRouche: OK, first of all, what we have is a general case of moral and intellectual degeneration throughout the whole system of the United States. There are individual exceptions to that pattern, but they are a very tiny minority. Look at the education system in California: California's education system is really an abomination, because they are destroying the minds of the students! And it becomes like a religion that they're devoted to.

Degeneracy starts in the schools, as with this text on monetarist economics.

We have some groups of circles in California, which we work with, and yes, they understand this. But the problem is, is that there's a need for a coherence among the people who do recognize that this is wrong, that what's going on is wrong, that the education system is wrong. But the difficulty is to get people to have confidence in themselves to be able to play a role of leadership which will move the society, move the people in the society, to improve themselves.

And that goes all through the country. Philadelphia's a mess; it's a horrible mess. Everybody who's there knows what the abuses are. And so that's the kind of thing we have to consider. And therefore, what I'm doing and what other people should be doing—those of us who understand how to organize society's behavior to get out of these kinds of messes—, *we have to mobilize ourselves to be the force that causes the desired effect to occur.*

Question: Good afternoon Lyndon. I want to wish you a very happy New Year; we're very happy to have you in this New Year. And I guess we're saying good riddance to the last year. But we did some work. The Manhattan Project was built last year and it advanced. So the question is, where are we going to go with it next, and I just wanted to ask you about,— well, we need to resurrect the ideas of Hamilton. New York is where he was; he came here, was brought here, because

he wanted to develop his mind; maybe he was brought here with the intention of having him play a role. But whatever it was, he had an uncanny creative power and he was able to figure out the natural laws behind the appearances, and maybe he got a good chance to see how the world economy functioned living on the outposts of the Empire.

Now Roosevelt tried to resurrect it, by making "Freedom from Want" a basic principle of his policy, which is also embedded in the principle of posterity that Hamilton bequeathed to us. So I'm just wondering, what is the best way to bring Hamilton to bear into the present, bring him back in spirit, and there are some attempts—there's a play called *Hamilton* which I understand is not very good ...

LaRouche: No!

Question: [follow-up] It has bad music. It has some interesting information, but the modality is pathetic. But what're we going to do ... it's really up to us, to figure out a way to bring Hamilton back into our minds and to resurrect these ideas. What principles do we need to focus on ...?

We Have a Solution

LaRouche: No, we have a solution. It's actually international. We have various parts of the planet which are sources of inspiration for mankind. The difficulties, the suffering, the problems, all these things are there. And what we have now, we have the sense of leadership. We lost the sense of leadership in the United States, at least so far recently; we've lost it. And we've lost it because of the Bushes, and Obama. Not just them, because they're only the agents of the forces which did it. Then, at the same time, we have a Congress which is half-witted, or one-quarter-witted. And so therefore, we have to stage a fight, we have to inject a kind of influence into this social process, to get some more people to do what they should.

I can tell you, from the experience we just had in the two performances, the musical events, that that expresses the kind of thing we needed to do! Those two sessions, on Saturday and Sunday, were the most blessed thing that has happened to the United States in recent history: Imagine about 1,000 people, children, the performers and so forth, all functioning! And this was a center of force, and it still *is* a force, from around Manhattan: It's a force which can resuscitate the United States. And it's located essentially in Manhattan. The effect of it can be spread, by influence, and should be. We have to mobilize the people of the United States, who represent that movement, which is now an established movement; it was an electrifying act! I mean, those two performances, Saturday and Sunday, those two events were an inspiration for mankind, first of all in Manhattan, and then for mankind.

It's things like that which you have to seize upon, because these become the infectious elements which you need, to create forces that spread; whereas in most other parts of the United States, there either is no development whatsoever, there's only backwardness, or there's fear.

And therefore, for me, this is what you have to do. We have one possibility; we have one possibility, in Manhattan, in the United States, that's the center. Manhattan as reflected in what happened in those two performances, *that* is the model. Now you've got to take that, use that as a source of influence and try to spread it, first of all in that area, to consolidate this, and then to spread it. That's our best shot.

Question: Happy New Years, Lyndon. K—W—from Brooklyn. I've been doing an online radio show for three years in April: Dennis has been on it; Daniel has been on it; most recently, Paul Gallagher from LaRouche PAC has been on it, and also I interviewed Yanis Varoufakis, former finance minister of Greece, because more and more people have been saying, as of late, what I saw and felt. And you know, we were trying to tell people, back in the seventies,— you know, I hear you talking a lot about the youth being degenerated, and I basically saw and felt, and was saying that in the early seventies: the breakdown of the family system.

I just wanted to mention what's recently been coming out about Exxon, and these other companies

Hermitage Museum, St. Petersburg, Russia

Uplifting mankind: The Return of the Prodigal Son by Rembrandt, drawn c. 1661-1669.

who knew about climate change and then were using their funding to quiet and deny their own science; and I feel like that's an epidemic, really, in our science, just being unhealthy and denying what's healthy and fit; and even the family system is doing the exact opposite of what is healthy and fit to their own children.

People Who Love Other People

LaRouche: Yes. Yes, that is absolutely true, and it has to be changed. It has to be changed. If we get people doing it, if we can get them to participate and agree to do that, that will help. And if you can spread it still further, that will help. This is not impossible; but there are very few people who are good prophets, shall we say; they're not very efficient at being prophets and therefore they don't succeed where they might have been able to succeed, because they were not developed.

You have lots of people who have an impulse toward good ideas, but they're not capable to deal with them effectively. And therefore, they don't win the effect which is necessary. And it's not a hopeless-for-all-time issue; it's a question of whether can we influence people to become decent people and good people? And that takes some work sometimes. But if you wander around demoralized because you don't get your own way, the way you think you should get your own way, that demoralization itself will make you destructive, a destructive force; because you are not responding to the potential, that you might be able to exert an influence which will inspire people to discover, in themselves, something which makes them more worthwhile as people.

People who love other people, who care about other people, people who care about other families, who care about the effects of life, who worry about the sick, who worry about these kinds of problems, and that kind of inspiration, the idea of making a contribution, which will make the society's circumstances better,—that's what it all starts with. And if you lose that, if you become disheartened and you're not willing to try to help, well you may not be able to succeed with some people. *But*, you can find other people, who *will* be responsive. And those people who *will* be responsive, become the germ of actually creating the effects we need.

What happened between Saturday and Sunday in the choruses, this *changed* the course of everything! It changed it! It worked! Now, the problem is, we've got to extend that, what was accomplished by those two concerts, we've got to extend that principle, and work from Manhattan and its surroundings to use that and spread it! To get the equivalent of 1,000 into a singing service like that, that is something significant. There's nothing in the United States, in any part of the United States—except some kind of little boolah-boolah, or some baseball or basketball nonsense—that can attract that number of people. And when you get children, accomplished performers, and an aggregate of 1,000 people between two places, back to back, you cannot possibly assume that everything is desperate. Which means that you've got to get your handle on the things that are not the causes of desperation.

Question: [follow-up] I want to say one more thing. People talk a lot about income equality and wealth and the "wealth gap," and how the top 0.1% owns whatever—42, or whatever the percentage of wealth compared to the bottom 90% of the people. But what I don't understand is, why do people measure wealth, and I feel that as long as we're going to measure wealth by something that man just kind of makes up out of thin air in a Petri dish, we're never going to fix life's problems. Real wealth should be measured by morality and what comes from nature and natural law, and not some fake thing that man creates out of nothing, which is actually more representative of death than actual wealth, so. I think—

LaRouche: Well, my reaction to that is, I know that we have an accelerating rate, of total collapse of the economy and possibilities of life, among people in the United States. There is no prosperity. There is only degeneration.

Because, you know, how do you get prosperity? Well, you have to get the human beings to develop practices which will create the prosperity. You don't get prosperity by stealing something. Some people think that; but they're only stealing from somebody else, and they're spreading the poverty, one way or the other, indirectly.

No, the problem is just exactly that: There is no great wealth. There may be people who are called "wealthy," but I can tell you that every person who is wealthy in the Wall Street sense, is hopelessly bankrupt right now! And totally bankrupt right now! So that's not something you have to worry about. You have to worry about the other side: How do you get these guys out of there, quick! Before more damage is done.

And therefore, the rate of death, the rate of degeneration and the approach to death through degeneration, among the people in the United States,— look, for example, people who are poorly employed, who used to have jobs that meant something, those jobs have now become deteriorated. They're marginal; they're degenerate; they're being thrown out of everything. They're dying! So there is *nothing good* in the system the way it's working now.

And the fact that you have something like this 1,000-person attendance between Saturday and Sunday,—this should inspire people by understanding what the lesson is that that represents. And that should be your source of confidence.

Comment: It's a proof of principle.

Crossing the Delaware

LaRouche: Yes, yes. That's it exactly.

And so, the point is, we should not be discouraged,

we should be *angry*, but not discouraged. Angry because of what is not done, or angry at that which is wrong and should not have been done. And what we want to do, is assemble people, to assemble among themselves as a team, and the best success we have had in this is in Manhattan, in the Manhattan area. It's the greatest success story we've had, recently. And what we have to do, is understand what that means, and then know how to interpret it. Then we become the prophets—of progress.

Metropolitan Museum of Art, New York City

Washington Crossing the Delaware, painted in 1851 by Emanuel Leutze (1816-1868).

Question: Good afternoon, Mr. LaRouche: It's P— from Connecticut—the only one. I put this together kind of rough. Our town representatives and a ranking Senator of the state of Connecticut have been sending us updates on how bad and out of control our state government is, and how frustrated and disgusted, and how helpless they are because they have no voice. Whatever they do to help us, is not heard.

So I came up with this: I wrote them a letter, all the representatives of our town and the Senator, and I said: "You need to tell the people the truth. We are in a catastrophical financial collapse, make no mistake, and this will be followed by thermonuclear war annihilation." I said, "Please, write to the people and explain, there is a viable solution to stop this, FDR's Banking Act of 1933, Glass-Steagall. Tell them to email, call, the three elected officials in the state capital and demand that they support and sign on to H.R. 381 and S. 1709. It's your commitment to the people to protect and to get them into the fight. Let's cross the Delaware now." [LaRouche laughs]

I did get a response. So I will work with them, and get all the constituents of Connecticut onboard. And we will hit them with a vast population of demands. Actually, we could just go up there and just remove them; that would. … [laughter]

LaRouche: Let me say: Look at the case of George Washington crossing the Delaware. Now, what was he doing? He made a strategic decision, on which the very continued existence of the United States depended. He made it in the most inclement area you could imagine, the worst weather conditions you could imagine. And he got the troops to mobilize, despite all of these conditions, to cross the Delaware, against the British forces, which were having a celebration out there, on the assumption that Washington would *never* interfere, with a Delaware passage.

So what happened is, Washington did it! And before anyone knew anything about it—they were trying to celebrate, they were half-drunk—they were all rounded up and shuffled off!

Now, that is important; Washington did that, it was a very risky thing for him to do, but he acted on the basis of reason, because he understood that the mentality of the soldiers, the British forces, was such that they had a way of behaving, but they understand Washington. Now, Washington had been a strategist in wars, in the Indian wars, and so he was very experienced with this kind of thing.

You remember the case where the Indians were about to sabotage and kill all these soldiers, and he knew what to do. Now, the fact that George Washington solved the problem, meant that he had a strategic capability that was more potent than these guys across the Delaware could ever have imagined. On the basis of that action rested the victory of the founding of the United States; without it there would have been no United States. The disaster would have been total.

So therefore, at this time, you're talking about as an option, and you have to make that option work. It means you have to get more support for it, to make sure it's going to succeed.

Question: [follow-up] We'll do that. And I thank you for bringing us onto the shore of the Delaware. [laughter]
LaRouche: Thank you!

Question: Hi, Mr. LaRouche, this is E—B— from the Bronx.
LaRouche: I met you some place!

Mankind is a Future Creature

Question: [follow-up] I'd like to ask you, among all the candidates that are running now for President, from the Democrats and the Republicans, is there any one candidate that you think would make a good President? And even if you don't think that one of them would make a good President, a great President, would you say that you would have to give him or her a chance to see what he or she does, when in office, if elected to the Presidency? Or are all of them not meeting your standards of what should be done?

LaRouche: What I think right now, under present conditions and the present trends, there is no possibility of a successful creation of a decent Presidency in the United States.

Now, the question is, how do we react, that being the case? Well, I always, in trying to do things like that,— but I don't stick any one thing; because I know that the future is not pre-fixed. The future is an effective force but it's not fixed. You see that,—for example, in the Russian case which our team has been looking over again recently. And yes, the option is there, but you haven't won anything yet, and there's no sign that you're going to win an election for him [Martin O'Malley] or for anyone else at this time, unless you can introduce a factor *which is not yet known*. And it has to be an effective one.

Now, my specialty is to always look at that problem. I never assume that there's any one fixed position, that will actually do the job. What you have to do, is you have to think ahead, into the future. You have to foresee what the rest of mankind cannot see, something from the future, and that's what I concentrate on. I know that the present is never the future.

But people think about being practical. They say "experience teaches us." And I say, "experience is bunk. It's only bad news, it's bunk." And therefore, unless people can organize a population, to discover a solution which has not heretofore been known to man,—most of the time, you will be defeated. And therefore, you have to always think of the future in active terms, not in what *might* be the case; you have to actually have a grip, a solid grip. And what often gets me upset about my own organization is they don't grasp that! If you don't know the future, don't try to run the organization! In military affairs and so forth, it is always the same thing: If you don't have a grip on the future, you will either lose the war, or the guy who had the ability to win the war will have been a damned fool, and will fail.

In other words, what mankind must do,—the future! Washington presented himself on the basis of the future. If you don't know what the future brings, you don't have any way of accomplishing anything toward the future. My whole experience in life has been always,— I know that the only thing that works, is the future. It has to be the real future.

The problem I have with my own organization is that. When I went to the jug, they lost that ability to see the future. They wanted to be practical! What do people say? "We've got to be practical." I say, "You're an idiot! You shouldn't be doing anything. If you think you're practical, you should be fired, or sent into some comfortable place where you won't be bothered very much. Because you're not going to create any progress, not real progress. People talk about progress, but what's the usual result of "progress," as promoted? Failure! Claims to success are usually failures.

So the question is,—it's known in military terms and other terms also: If you don't know the future, and the future is not the right choice, you ain't a leader, or you shouldn't be! And my problem is, I have people who don't like what I do, because I want the future! I don't want some cheap imitation of a past disguised as the future. I don't want past affairs; that I don't want. I want a future. I want a creative future, and I want it to be a workable future, a necessary future.

But most people don't know that. They say, "You want to be successful; well, if you do this and you do this and you do this, these patterns, you will be successful." I say, "you will not be successful! You'll be a

Creativity in action: the Experimental Superconducting Tokamak in China.

creating discovery, but that's what it is. Don't you realize that the United States has been an historic failure, mostly, since Franklin Roosevelt was thrown out of office by the FBI? The FBI threw him out of office [in 1944]. Then he died later. But the consequence was a destruction. And we have had almost *no successful President in the United States*, who lived very long.

If you cannot create the future, you cannot solve these kinds of problems. And my dedication is precisely such, that I don't like to get involved in anything which I believe is not the future. You have to create the future! And that's the meaning of mankind.

Unfortunately, in educational institutions today,—unlike Einstein, Einstein did see the future; most of the so-called deductionist scientists did not. They failed. Look, these two musical events on Saturday and Sunday in sequence, do you realize that that is the kind of thing which seems in one sense to be an old thing, an old idea; but if you look at it carefully, it's a creation process? It's bringing into play an *idea*, which mankind thought it *had lost*; but mankind then discovered a suspicion—only a good suspicion—that there was a future behind that pair of events. But it was only a good idea, only a promise. You have to make it real.

No, you don't get things by this idea of lucky this, lucky that, lucky this; or even good ideas. You've got to get something beyond that: A creative force, and this is a military question; it's also other kinds of questions. But, frankly, I have no confidence in popular opinion, none at all. Why? Because it's popular. What we need is the future, the future of mankind, the progress of mankind; the kind of progress that mankind has never known before. And under these kinds of conditions, in which the whole culture of the trans-Atlantic region, is

failure! Probably a disaster." And the trouble is, you've got to foresee the nature of mankind.

Mankind is a future creature! Human beings are not animals. The identity of a human being is as a being who discovers things, such as principles,—Einstein for example,—who discovers *principles* which mankind has not really understood before. These are fresh ideas. Principles are fresh ideas. And it's only a person with fresh ideas of that nature—like George Washington's practices, and Alexander Hamilton's practices, for example—who achieves success.

The Meaning of Mankind

If you're trying to imitate something, if you're trying to adduce something from experience, you're never going to create the future. And what we're dealing with now, we have to accomplish the future! China is creating a future; Russia is creating a future. It's actually being created, a real future. In Europe? There's nothing,—hopeless!

If you cannot create the future, you ain't human, or you haven't achieved it. And the point of these kinds of discussions is to evoke a conception of a workable idea of the future. You may have good sentiments, and good views, and those are elements which are the ground of collapsing! Disintegrating! The crucial thing is how do we get insight into what is the future.

Now, I think O'Malley is probably the only Presidential prospect, who I know now, who might just be competent to become a President. I'm not sure he's going to be able to do that; but I think it's that kind of outlook, because all the other candidates I know for President or similar kinds of positions, are failures; most of them are failures! I know they're disasters from the beginning!

And what's important in life is to be able to create the future, like Einstein.

Question: [follow-up] Thank you, Mr. LaRouche. Now I understand. I get what you mean. But you said there may be one candidate that could be a good President, and you mentioned O'Malley.

LaRouche: I tell you: The others all have such serious defects, all the others I know have such serious defects, I don't want them in the territory! [laughter] We're looking for what O'Malley might be able to do.

Speed: We're going to take one final question, Lyn.

Question: Hi Lyndon, it's K— from the Bronx. I was picking up some reading material very, very recently that came from Walter Russell, who wrote in the 1950s; and he wanted to raise the culture and the mentality of mankind, and he made reference to New York City. He said, that of the eight million people in New York City there were 7,000 who wanted the silences of nature and sought the beauties of music. The other 8 million wanted the noise and the jazz. I just thought you would find that interesting.

What I wanted to speak about is, Spain. Spain has recently had their elections, which confirm that southern Europe is going through a political earthquake. The tremors first destroyed the mainstream parties in Greece; this autumn Portugal was plunged into unprecedented political turmoil; now Spain. Italy sits on the brink of a major banking crisis. The voters of southern Europe are in open revolt against Germany imposing austerity. Can the EU survive 2016? Across Europe upstart parties are breathing down the necks of their established rivals.

How do you see the future of Europe and the relationships with Germany?

LaRouche: Well, everything is in jeopardy in the trans-Atlantic region as far I'm concerned. Egypt is interesting. It's a successful society, and in general it is a leading agency; Russia, presently, is a leading agency; Spain and Portugal of course are disasters, and there's no hope. France is a disaster from my standpoint; there are some elements, but the overall characteristic of the government of France, is that the government morally is not capable of doing its duty. There are people in France, if we remove some of the governing people, you could probably get a government which might be functional. But as long as you have the variety of governments, of Presidencies and so forth that we have in France today, you have to look back at the history between what happened earlier, in history, and you have to look at the fact that France is largely corrupted.

Now, I've known some people in France who were important people. But they weren't able to sustain the fight; Charles de Gaulle himself was bounced out; and the old crowd came back in again. A friend of mine who was running as a candidate for some years, repeatedly, but he was always bounced out.

The Miracle of Manhattan

So therefore, you're in that kind of situation, France is useless, so far. It would be a *miracle*, if France produced anything at this point.

Greece is being destroyed; it's being crushed. The nations in that territory are being ruined! And if you want to get good fun, you have to work with the desperation,—think in terms of Russia. Russia, today, is a positive institution; China's a positive institution. There are other nations in Asia which are positive institutions.

But the trans-Atlantic region? There is no stability, no secured stability, in any place in the trans-Atlantic community. It's finished, in its present form, unless an intervention comes from China and Russia, and India, and so forth. Then the whole planet might come back.

The problem essentially is, the rot is the British Empire. And the British Empire is a product of the Satanic evil which crushed the Renaissance. Then all the things that have happened, in terms of positive development, have suffered in totality, from the kinds of omissions in these matters.

I'm not a pessimist, but I know that there is no good security, *unless you can create a future*, a true future. Not a projection of the present, but something which has never been done before, by anyone. And that's the only way you can solve this problem. And that's what

Seminal mind of the Italian Renaissance, Dante Alighieri (1265-1321), shown in a fresco in the Chapel of San Brizio in the Orvieto Cathedral.

I'm devoted to.

That's why I despise practical people! Why? Because I know they're not useful. They're doing the same old, same old thing; they're coming up with a new version of the same old, same old,—the old, dirty underwear, you know? And I don't think that's very productive.

But I think that we can assemble ourselves and look into what is the actual future of mankind,—the idea that there is a future! We used to understand that. But then, when Bertrand Russell got into power in the beginning of the Twentieth Century, then the idea of progress was *crushed*! And has been crushed and corrupted ever since. And what you have in Manhattan,—that's a miracle. And I think that miracle is one source of hope for mankind.

What we did in those two performances on Saturday and Sunday is an example of what could be the future. And I'm optimistic about it. That I'm optimistic about. The other stuff, I would warn people against.

Speed: So we're at the end, Lyn, and we're following your advice: We are going to omit any other questions, especially enunciated by myself. You've already said several times what you think about Manhattan. I don't know if you have anything in summary, but I will

say one thing about the music: We're getting all sorts of responses; we have an Italian choral director who wants to engage our chorus in a project to learn *Va Pensiero*, the way she says it should be done; because it's a prayer of slaves, and it's a prayer of revolution.

LaRouche: Yes.

Speed: So in any case, we're getting some interest from the people who know the art, and I think it's going to be interesting. I think you'll be seeing some of them here, actually, perhaps next week, or the following week. But I'd like to ask if you have anything other than what you've already said, in summary, that you'd like to convey to us?

LaRouche: I'd like to see your voice in better condition! [laughter] And you better do something about that, quickly!

Speed: [laughs] All right, since you have no intention of behaving, [laughter] we'll conclude the session today by thanking you for starting us off in the New Year in the right way!

LaRouche: OK, have fun!

This Crisis Is No Act of Nature— It's the Result of Bad Policy

by Helga Zepp-LaRouche, chair of the German political party Civil Rights Movement Solidarity (BueSo) and founder of the Schiller Institutes

The BueSo chairwoman presented the following video message for the New Year on the party's website on Jan. 1, 2016.

Dear Fellow Citizens!

Let me begin by wishing you a good and peaceful New Year!

But whether it turns out that way very much depends upon all of us. Many people sense that we are now in an existential crisis for civilization. This crisis, however, is not a natural phenomenon, but rather the result of bad policy; which means we can change the situation.

Today, January 1, 2016, a new law goes into effect throughout the European Union— the so-called "bail-in" law. This is the Cyprus Model, which the head of the Euro Group, Joeren Dijsselbloem, in March of 2013 demanded be applied to all of Europe: namely, that bank customers and creditors share in the costs of banks' bankruptcies. This policy was carried out in Cyprus at the time, and then in Spain, and recently in Portugal and Italy. The "bail-in" law signifies that in the case of banks' insolvencies, the depositors and stockholders have their funds expropriated to recapitalize banks which really should be closed. This is thievery, plain and simple.

After the financial crash of 2008, the governments of the G20 nations did absolutely nothing to shut down the casino economy, but rather pumped trillions of dollars (in the double digits) into the trans-Atlantic system through the so-called bailout. This converted private gambling debts into state indebtedness.

Today the "too big to fail" banks—which are allegedly too big to be allowed to fail—are around 40% larger than they were in 2008, and a new financial crash

BueSo

Helga Zepp-LaRouche addressing German citizens by video on Jan. 1, 2016.

is already underway; hedge funds and banks have already gone bankrupt; a wave of insolvency is in store especially for companies involved in shale gas and oil, which will unleash a meltdown of the outstanding derivatives contracts.

Allegedly, bank deposits of up to 100,000 euros are secure under the "bail-in" law. But in the case of only four bankrupt regional banks in Italy, the resources of the Italian deposit insurance funds were insufficient, and thousands of people lost everything, with two retirees committing suicide as a result. If this provision is applied throughout the rest of Europe and the United States—where it already exists in the so-called Dodd-Frank bill—there will be mass death hitting, above all, the poor, old, and sick.

The problem is that the laws of the EU, as well as those of the U.S. Congress, were decided upon under the diktat of the City of London and Wall Street, which are only concerned with defending the speculative wealth of those who benefit from the casino economy. The line that "bail-in" is necessary to spare the taxpayers the costs of future financial crises is an open lie. Because along with the "cost-sharing"—that is, the expropriation of the banks' creditors—it is planned to resort to "bail-outs" again: that is, ultimately the commitment of state funds, in order to save the holders of the derivative contracts. Nevertheless, even the combination of "bail-in" and "bail-out" will not suffice to "save" the outstanding derivatives of approximately two trillion euros, because the latter are greater by orders of magnitude than the monies that can be used to save them.

Leading politicians and EU bureaucrats, such as German Economics Minister Wolfgang Schäuble, European Central Bank head Mario Draghi, President of the European Commission Jean-Claude Juncker, and Dijsselbloem, would have us believe that we must accept this logic in order to guarantee the "stability of the markets." But it's criminal to insist that people accept something which is tantamount to their committing suicide. In Italy the people affected have realized what this policy means, and there is already a revolt underway against it.

The Solution

There is a solution.

In all the European countries and the United States, we must immediately do what Franklin D. Roosevelt did in 1933 as a solution to the financial crisis at that time: We must institute the Glass-Steagall/banking separation law, which will mean closing down the City of London, Wall Street, and the entire casino section of the trans-Atlantic financial sector. We don't need gambling which results in mass murder!

In its place, we must create a credit system on the basis of the principles established by Alexander Hamilton, the first Treasury Secretary of the United States. Friedrich List further developed these ideas which, along with those of Abraham Lincoln's adviser Henry C. Carey, provided the basis for Otto von Bismarck's industrial revolution. These ideas were also the foundation for FDR's policies and for the role of the Reconstruction Bank (Kreditanstalt für Wiederaufbau) in the German economic miracle after the Second World War.

There is already a strategic approach to overcome

China Radio International

Chinese President Xi Jinping gives his New Year's address to the nation.

the financial crisis, as well as the refugee crisis: China has presented its New Silk Road program (which already involves some 60 nations), based on a concept of economic cooperation among all nations of the world—a so-called "Win-Win Strategy." This is to the mutual advantage of all the countries participating in the reconstruction of infrastructure and comprehensive development. This means that the Chinese economic miracle of the last 30 years can be a model for all countries in the world.

The region where this is most urgently needed is obviously Southwest Asia, the entire region from Afghanistan to the Mediterranean, from the Caucasus to the Arabian Sea. Many of these countries have been "bombed back into the Stone Age" on the basis of lies (such as Saddam Hussein's alleged weapons of mass destruction), and have been reduced to rubble and ashes. We need a reconstruction program for this entire region, which can only be implemented if the concept of the New Silk Road is extended to this region: that is, integrated infrastructure; greening of the deserts through producing massive amounts of fresh water; reconstruction of destroyed cities and building new ones; and setting up industry and agriculture.

This is the only way to abate the flood of refugees, by creating a real prospect of a future for them in the countries from which they are fleeing war, terror, starvation, and poverty.

The cooperation at the Vienna Conference, at which Russia, China, and the United States, among others, are sitting down at one table, is a step in the right direction.

But after the military action, an economic reconstruction plan—a Silk Road Marshall Plan, if you will—must be on the agenda.

China and the BRICS countries are already creating a totally new banking system, to exclusively provide investment for the real economy: the Asian Infrastructure Investment Bank (AIIB), which is open to all countries; the New Development Bank of the BRICS (NDB); the Shanghai Cooperation Organization Bank; the New Silk Road Development Bank; the Maritime Silk Road Development Fund; and the Bank of the South Asian Association for Regional Cooperation—to name only a few.

Once we in Europe and the United States have put into effect the Glass-Steagall banking separation system, we will be able to work with these Asian banks not only in the reconstruction of Southwest Asia, but also to develop the African continent at long last, and thus eliminate another root cause of the refugee crisis.

A New Era for Mankind

This year, 2016, is the year in which we must shift the fate of mankind in a positive direction—and we can do it! We must replace the geopolitics which led to two world wars in the Twentieth Century—and threatens today to lead to a third, this time thermonuclear world war, and thus the extinction of mankind—with the common aims of mankind. Or, as Chinese President Xi Jinping put it yesterday in his New Year's Address: "Let us work together to build a community of common destiny of all mankind."

In Germany we have at our disposal a great treasure-trove which we can bring to this common destiny. That is a renaissance of our Classical culture—from Bach to Beethoven and Brahms, from Lessing and Schiller to von Humboldt, and all the great thinkers whose ideas are required for a new international community, for a new level of evolution of mankind—such as Nicholas of Cusa, Johannes Kepler, Gottfried Leibniz, and Albert Einstein, to name only a few.

The dangers with which we are confronted in 2016 are immense. But if we concentrate on realizing the solutions outlined here—and I would ask you to actively help us to do so—then we will be able to ring in a new era for mankind.

What we need, above all, is an optimistic image of man, which understands man as good and capable of unlimited improvement, as well as a fond love for mankind.

I wish you, and all of us, a happy New Year!

Every Day Counts In Today's Showdown To Save Civilization

That's why you need EIR's **Daily Alert Service**, a strategic overview compiled with the input of Lyndon LaRouche, and delivered to your email 5 days a week.

For example: On November 5, EIR's Daily Alert featured Lyndon LaRouche's warning that Obama can and must be removed immediately, to avoid Obama's push for thermonuclear confrontation with Russia. That issue identified The Drone Papers put out by Glenn Greenwald's The Intercept as the Pentagon Papers of 2015—damning Barack Obama as a mass murderer, and providing the evidence for his Constitutional removal from office.

That edition also featured EIR's exclusive report on a hearing called by Rep. John Conyers on Capitol Hill to expose the dangers represented by Obama's actions—a hearing all but suppressed by other media.

This is intelligence you need to act on, if we are going to survive as a nation and a species. Can you really afford to be without it?

THURSDAY, NOVEMBER 5, 2015

EIR Daily Alert Service

EIR DAILY ALERT SERVICE P.O. BOX 17390, WASHINGTON, DC 20041-0390

- Dump Obama Now or Face Thermonuclear Holocaust
- Extraordinary Capitol Hill Event Warns of Obama Thermonuclear War Provocations against Russia
- Rep. Tulsi Gabbard: Unlawful for U.S. To Wage War in Syria
- Satanic Environmentalist Offensive Launched in U.S.
- O'Malley Campaign Support Grows in Iowa, Key Democrats Say
- Behind the New York Times Headlines on 'Death in Middle Age'
- QE Inflated Wall Street, Screwed Main Street—Says Wall Street
- Russian Defense Ministry Coordinating with Syrian Opposition against ISIS
- Frontex: Arrest Illegal Immigrants!
- Bavaria Considering a Constitutional Case against Merkel
- U.S.-Russian Communications Test over Syria
- Malaysia and ASEAN Stand Up To Obama's Threats over South China Sea
- Barenboim's Orchestra Plays Mozart for Peace in the Middle East

EDITORIAL

Dump Obama Now or Face Thermonuclear Holocaust

The Law, the Citizenry And the Government

Immediately below are selected excerpts taken from two live dialogues with Lyndon LaRouche: his discussion with the LaRouche PAC Policy Committee on December 28, 2015, and his national Fireside Chat on December 30, 2015.

From the Policy Committee Discussion

Lyndon LaRouche: All right,—we have one of the most crucial moments in history for the whole planet. That is, what's happening through the international system, the United States, the British system, and so forth, Europe in general, is terrible. China is less affected directly, but is indirectly affected. So as of this time, we have entered a period in which the intention is to reduce the population's resources to effect virtual mass murder.

That is what is in process, unless the Obama Administration is ordered to prevent this thing from happening. So the existence of Obama as President of the United States is, in part, the major issue for life of all human beings on this planet. But! In particular, the United States is responsible.

Now, in other parts of the planet, certain parts of Asia, for example,—Europe is in a mess. Europe is in a terrible mess. It's a terrible threat. The threat against the people of Europe is monstrous, right now! And I know this material directly, so let's not debate it in detail. The point also is that China and India and so forth, and Asian nations, are also implicitly threatened by this thing. But the main thing is that the major threat is in the trans-Atlantic region, right now! And we're looking at a threat of *massive death* of human beings over the first days, and into the next days. And that's what is happening right now.

The question is, can we get Obama thrown out of the Presidency now, in time to avoid an absolute disaster?....

Diane Sare: ... Part of the challenge we face is the very deep pessimism and despair of the population. And partly that is challenging to overcome, because in the last 50 years, the culture has so degraded that people look within themselves, and they have a hard time locating a certain quality of emotional strength, and emo-

St. Paul, whose epistles dealt profoundly with the question of Natural Law, in a 1633 painting by Rembrandt.

tional determination, to persevere whatever the obstacles. And I think in that regard, what we saw with the incredible response to the performances of Handel's Messiah in Manhattan and Brooklyn, is people grappling for something greater, something which they haven't known about themselves for some time, that will give the strength necessary to actually persevere and to resist the incredible degradation of tolerating and going along with this.

The Wrong Laws

LaRouche: We have a whole century after the Renaissance; the collapse of the Renaissance and that whole century and beyond, has been the kind of destruction which has occurred. We have had over a century of this kind of thing over much of the planet. It's mass murder. So what's the law? The law is, mass murder is illegal....

... And this is again the same British animal. The British animal has been the dominant factor, and the British animal is Obama! Obama is a creation of the British system; that was the way it was done.

And what was before then, the Bush family,—well, the Bushes should have been burned.

But we're at this kind of point: this is reality. And everything that we can do that is right in nature, should be done. Law is not supreme when it violates the *principle* of law.

Ben Deniston: And I think that can go to what you're saying on natural law. That the effect of policies that go against the natural necessity of the existence of a growing economy, ends with this result.

LaRouche: I think your point on natural law is the crucial point to emphasize.

Bill Roberts: ... As Michael raised earlier, this crisis is the will of Obama, when he intervened to impose Dodd-Frank and block Glass-Steagall. That was an intervention on behalf of creating this crisis. So it's not just a financial crisis that Congress finds itself admitting to, but that this was created by the cultural norm that they accepted, the degraded state. And so that has to be taken on, top down.

LaRouche: Well, there's another, deeper issue here in terms of history. The problem is, that we take laws and we use laws which are wrong laws, and we don't understand what the real law is. They say, "well, human beings have made a choice; that is, ordinary society's human beings have made a choice, and this, therefore, is law."

Now, that is not true! It never was true. Particularly when you look at the appeasers of evil in relatively modern history, that is, since the Renaissance. And what happened with the Renaissance was the introduction immediately afterward,—they shut it down, and they created degeneration. They created mass murder! That's what happened.

Now, what's the point? The idea of the law is not the true law; that's the problem. That was the problem then, after the closing-down of the Renaissance, and we had a big struggle to get something in Europe and elsewhere, which was not evil. And we fought evil repeatedly. And we don't say that the law,—the letter of the law as provided by some people because they happen to be in power,—that that defines the principle of law for the human species! In other words, **the other law is a responsibility of mankind's security and development, and progress: that is the law!** And if that law is defied, if that is defied, then the crime has been committed!

Matthew Ogden: You know, I think Putin addressed that very clearly in his speech to the United Nations a few months ago, and then also more recently, where he's taken the question of what is the standard of international law, and how that's been violated repeatedly by, for example, the Bush and Obama administrations, with the overthrowing of sovereign governments and the imposing of the will of one nation on another nation, which is a definition of aggressive warfare.

That's the kind of thing that the United Nations was set up in order to prevent in the aftermath of World War II, which was really a major reason why Franklin Roosevelt mobilized the entire American people, in alliance with the Russians at that time, to defeat what was coming out as fascism in Europe in the 1930s. There is a standard of international law, and there's a standard which the United Nations is intended to represent, and that's exactly what Putin and Xi Jinping and others have been addressing very clearly in their recent interventions on that question.

What Real Law Is

LaRouche: But there's a higher question here, which I've raised occasionally, which is not raised usually; when it comes to technicalities, it's not raised; it's not treated. The problem is that mankind cannot really

FIGURE 1

Energy Consumption Per Person and Population Growth

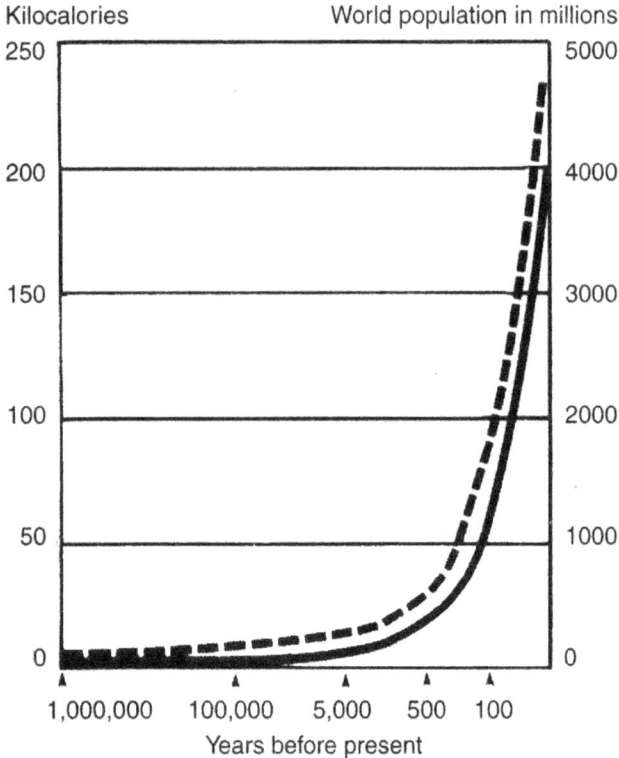

21st Century Science & Technology

One aspect of the natural law of progress is the requirement for increased energy consumption per capita. This graphic depicts the leap in population growth (solid line) that follows the increase in energy available per capita (dashed line)—an increase achieved by man's creative inventions of new technologies.

make the law! That is, mankind does not, by mankind's own authority as such—by terms of individual members of societies—does not really make the law. **Because the law is the principle of the progress of the human species,** and if the human species is not progressing in its development and its fruition, then the law has been violated! And that's where the problem lies.

You look at the terrible things that have happened, under which various Renaissances have been crushed; look at what the mass murder was of that. Now we're talking about a mass murder problem right now. What we're talking about is the policy of the United States government right now, at least under the current President and the preceding two presidential terms: mass murder!

So therefore, there is no law which justifies the existence of the people who do that thing! And therefore, you don't say, "there's a technical law, there's a law on the books." That is not the law! Because the worst, the most Satanic forces on the planet, have been the law! That's how it worked!

And the point is that mankind is answerable to a higher law, because mankind is not an Earthling! Mankind is based on a principle which is not that of Earthlings. It is the responsibility of mankind to develop future populations which are more fitting. The assumption is that every generation should be moving progressively, in terms of its natural law, and the natural law is the improvement, the self-improvement of the human species. And only mankind has the power to do that.

So when somebody comes in, in government, and says "We're government, we have a law." Who made the law? Who says it's the law? What's the law?

Well, you had in Christianity, for example,—under Christianity what happened was the idea of law governing mankind *per se*, and that's the higher law. The higher law is that mankind must produce next generations which are superior, for the purpose of mankind, for the progress of mankind. And mankind must rise to higher levels of achievement: That's God's law! And we call it God's law, not this petty law that people gossip about.

But that's what it is. Mankind has to make progress, and the obligation of law, among nations, is progress for mankind's condition; better intellectual development; newer, higher levels of knowledge; higher levels of achievement; higher meanings of the existence of mankind, of successive generations of mankind.

And that's the law, that's the real law. The technical law, the book law,—that is not the law. The law is that mankind must progress in its nature. That, you know, people die; all right, fine. What's the law? Well, did they get better people produced in their families? Were their families able to be progressive in going to higher levels of achievement for mankind? Are we not responsible to take care of the Galaxy, for example? We are responsible!

So who's going to shut that law down? The law is that mankind must progress, that mankind's achievement must progress, by that higher standard. You know, we've even got other cases on that thing.

Ogden: Well, one thing that comes to mind is Alex-

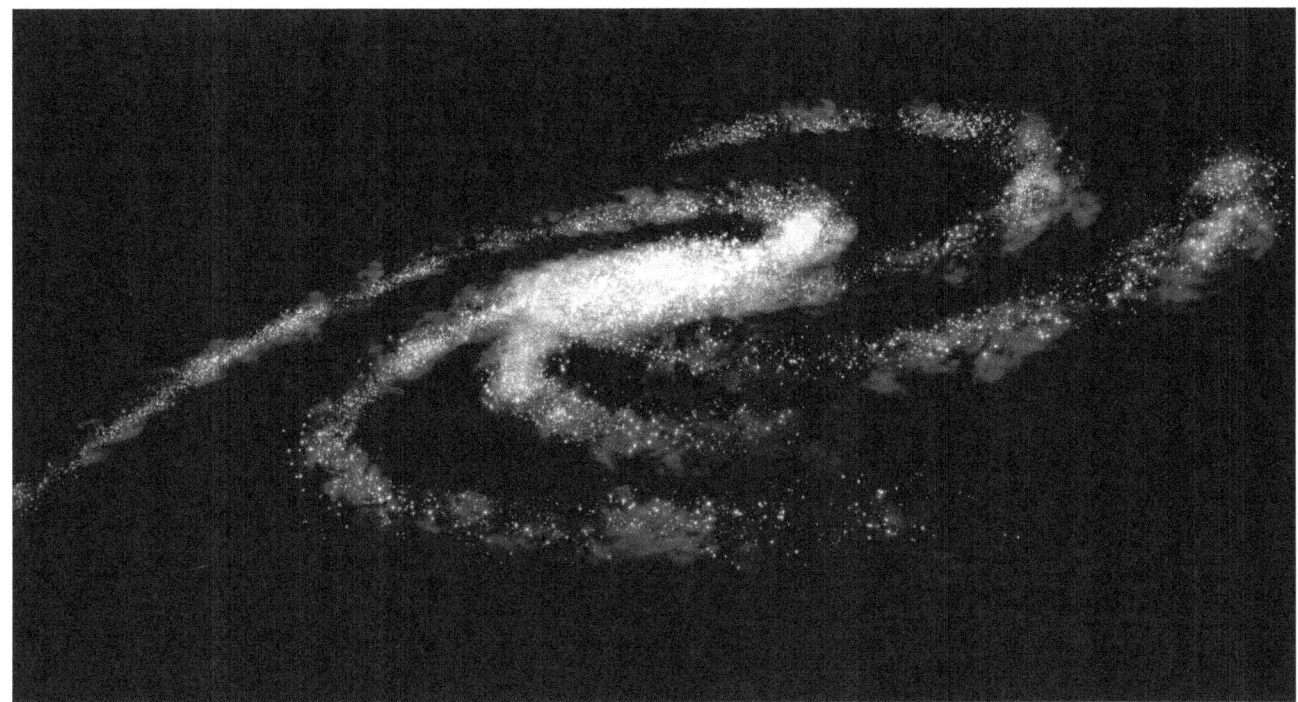

An artist's impression of mankind's true home, the Milky Way Galaxy.

NASA

ander Hamilton, absolutely. That was absolutely the discussion of Alexander Hamilton and his associates in the *Federalist Papers* and elsewhere, the question of natural law. That was the birth of our nation, based on that idea.

LaRouche: But the point is, what about the Galaxy? Mankind is responsible to improve upon the Galaxy; that's implicit. Who could take that away? Who has the right to take that away? Who has the authority to take that away?

Deniston: I think this message needs to go to the Pope, pretty quickly.

LaRouche: I think the Pope should probably be put into suspension. His existence should be in some kind of suspension. He should not be Pope-ular.

Deniston: Well, the precedent of Cusa really sticks out in my mind. Because you see his work on science, also his work on the nation-state, the idea of a government of a republic,—it flows from the discovery he made, a higher conception about mankind's creative mission and existence in the universe. And that was the basis then, for him to develop and take further conceptions about how must society organize itself to facilitate this progress.

The Principle of Law

LaRouche: You have to look at Brunelleschi, too. Brunelleschi was very important in this; the Renaissance would not have occurred without Brunelleschi. It was going to be one of the old, usual kinds of systems of government. And Brunelleschi forced it, and what happened was that the Renaissance as such was continued.

But then that got crushed! It got crushed in the beginning of the next century, which became an evil thing, just like what we're talking about now! That's what happened after that, after the end of that century: It came down. And that is what happened in the various stages of Renaissance efforts after that point.

No, there is a higher law, and we have to really specify there is a higher law for mankind. And mankind is not limited to being an Earthling; that's also the case. Mankind goes out to higher levels of achievement, beyond what we call nature, natural nature. And the development of mankind is through the progress of the development of mankind's ability to create, and that is the directly pertinent precedent for law. Are you creating a level of achievement for subsequent generations? That's the issue!

And this thing is Satanic! And that's the only way to say it: "This is entirely Satanic, directly Satanic." That Obama and everything he represents is a Satanic personality, and therefore should not be considered human.

Because the right to have rights depends upon your humanity. And humanity is something which is dependent upon of the birth of new generations and development and progress. And that's the principle of law, and that's the only law that mankind has ever been able to define. Does mankind become a better, more powerful force for good, in the history of mankind? That's the issue!

And this is Satanic! And we have to use the word Satanic, to describe those who are making these orders. You say, "Well this is the law"—well, you are operating under Satanic law. We are under the order of anti-Satanic law.

And we have to do it that way. If you don't do it, if you don't go to this question of what's a higher principle, and you say, "Well, assume we have a human order of principle."... But that's not the principle; the existence of mankind does not depend upon these kinds of caprices! It depends entirely upon the progress of mankind as a species! And mankind is the only power that has a willful capability of improvement in species.

White House/Tina Hager

George W. Bush during his meeting with Saudi Crown Prince Abdullah at the Crawford Ranch in April 2002.

From the Fireside Chat

Lyndon LaRouche: But the crucial thing here, of course, is that we have to understand that we're working under a threat of extinction. By that I mean the fact that the typical American can have his job, his life rights, all kinds of things taken away from him in the course of even weeks and months. That's what's on now. That's what's coming from Obama, it's coming from his program. It's coming from the British Empire, the British Empire as such.

It means also some Satanic elements, like 9/11, the 9/11 crisis: Here we had a number of citizens, especially concentrated in Manhattan. And they were subjected to mass killing, especially in the southern part of Manhattan; one spot in Washington, mass murder. The mass murder has never been uncovered. The Congress of the United States, the institutions that go with the Congress of the United States, have always suppressed as much as possible the fact of what happened in 9/11.

What was 9/11? I'll tell you what 9/11 is, and it's

what you're going to think about. What happened was that the British Empire, which was working with the Saudis, Saudi agents as well as the British agents,—and they ran an operation which invaded the United States, in their own operation, and they created a mass murder operation in that time, during the attacks on particularly Manhattan.

Now, this thing was going on already, it had been. It was run by the British and the British Monarchy in cohesion with the Saudis. These are our mortal enemies. And that has to be remembered. There has never been justice delivered to the victims, to the memory of the victims, of those who died in Manhattan by Saudi agents and British agents. Never!

What Is the United States?

But since that time, there's always been a moot argument that we must not offend the Saudis and the British, the ones who murdered our citizens. And it means all the terrorist screwballs and so forth, which have come up under the Bush family and Obama. And the name of Bush, and of Obama, is the most hateful thought which any honest American can experience. And therefore, the important thing we have to say: The members of Congress who sanctified the suppression of the 9/11 information are treasonous agents working against the United States, in effect, now.

And you want to digest that a little bit, because here we are: We were attacked by the British. It was a British-Saudi oil business, and this is the thing that led to 9/11. And the Presidency of the United States, the majority of the forces of the Congress, and other people involved in this sort of thing, along with the British all along,—they committed warfare, in effect, against the United States. And those members of Congress who still cover up for what the Saudis did and what the British did in 9/11,—these people are not members of our government; they're only traitors.

And the time has come, we've got to clean this thing up. The first step we have to take: we have to force the Congress, in its shame, to lift the 9/11 ban. Until that time, the United States has not been honored by its Presidents, by its leading representatives in the Congress, and other agents. It has to be done now.

And now we're facing a great danger to the people of the United States, a great danger; one greater than anything most of them have ever thought of. And therefore, we have to—as people—we have to force our government to do the right thing, and stop covering up the intrinsic criminality, intrinsic to the British system and to the British system's golliwog, Saudi Arabia. Saudi Arabia and the British Monarchy are one piece, two parts of the same piece. They're both evil. And those who are acting to support 9/11, are complicit with evil, not only against the United States and the people of the United States but against humanity in general.

We've got to clean the mess up. And some people will enjoy doing that, especially some people whose families came from the southern quarter of Manhattan.

Question: [Describes how an employee of a Congressman's office became fascinated with the Manhattan choral process, after discussion with a young LaRouche organizer.] But I just wanted to fill you in on this, and hear what you have to respond, because it seems to me they need this just as much as the rest of the citizenry does,—to hear what we're doing, and to see it uplift them, and we should invite them along as well.

LaRouche: I think you've got a very good beginning there, a keystone effort. Because what needs to be understood, is avoided; that people will try to limit their discussions to things that they think are acceptable, or in some way they have a special attitude about them. When the problem is that we have to have a population mobilized, by itself in a sense, and by whatever we can contribute to make that happen; for the people of the

United States to take charge of the United States, of the people of the United States.

In other words, the problem is that the typical reaction is the idea of, "we're only amateurs, and we have to listen to the higher authority of higher elected people or elected officials" of that type. And the problem is that people do not have the psychology, in themselves, to realize that they cannot just simply ask funny questions of admirable people. We have to realize that we have to get our citizens in like soldiers. It doesn't mean they're taking guns or something,—they are like soldiers, they are part of an army; an army of citizens, and as an army of citizens whose power is to chastise and inspire the citizenry in general, and especially so-called authorities in high places.

That has to be the principle. This idea, "This guy's a bigshot, he's around all the world and so forth," that doesn't really sell anything, really, to anyone who understands reality. Yes, there is a reason to appreciate the achievements of some people in the discoveries they've made, and the fact that they may also be teachers, as well as leaders in a Congress or something like that, or officials in general.

But the point is, there has to be a reciprocal relationship between the ordinary citizens and the medium-level citizen and so forth, and the leadership. There has to be a process which is not a "your taste, my taste, his flavor, her flavor," this sort of thing. That's not the way. You have to bring people together, and bring them as groups from all walks of life, so to speak, to digest among themselves, in their discussion, and in the cross-discussion with other groups and similar groups; there has to be a commonality of development, of determining what kind of ideas should be promoted, and what role these ideas should contribute.

And that issue is where we've lost it in the United States in general. Very few people in the United States, as citizens or potential citizens, have ever been able to understand what the principle of Congress must be; what the United States is. Most people will talk about the United States, but they don't know what it is, and they never knew what it was. And that's what we have to fix.

What is Citizenship?

Question: Now, I have a question from a gentleman who hopefully heard what you just said, but it's along similar lines, communicated through the Internet. He asks: "Why has Obama been allowed to stay in office

creative commons/Daderot

"The Lexington Minuteman," a sculpture of Captain John Parker done by Henry Hudson Kitson and erected in 1900.

this long and has destroyed America without question? The spineless Congress and Senate hadn't gone against him nor denied his executive orders; why are they all afraid of that weasel?"

LaRouche: Okay, he's absolutely correct in placing the problem exactly there. The problem essentially is that the idea of freedom of the citizen is the right of the citizen to participate in election, the process of election, to participate in the discussion of policy; not someone who comes out like a beggar, saying "Please, Mr. Wiseguy, tell me what the news is?" Well, that's not very good influence.

You have to bring the people together. Now admittedly, during the first seven presidential terms of the United States after George Washington, this principle was not really understood well. And we had one good President after that, a great President. Then he was kicked out office after this crucial one term. And after that, there was a run-down up to Abraham Lincoln's role, there was a rundown of mostly fakers, in the name of Presidents. And we had big trouble with this, of course, with the Southerners, because that was an extension of that problem.

We never had a unified United States since that time, since the beginning,—for instance, since the death of Alexander Hamilton, Washington's service in particular, as President; then there were a few good things, plus terrible mistakes. You cannot say that at that time, there was much of anything of solidarity among citizens. There were a few times, you know, people would,—well, the Civil War was an important struggle. The losers were still losers, for the most part, and their progeny were generally also losers, like the others.

But the United States has not been a clean operation. It has not been a united nation, not since just the beginning: Alexander Hamilton and President Washington, that was the beginning of only a Presidency. But, since that time, ups and downs, ups and downs.

And the United States has had British influence coming in, other kinds of foreign influence coming in, foreign influences from France; foreign influence from Britain, and from other quarters.

So the United States has never really been, except in momentary cases, like in fighting the Civil War ..., there's not really been much solidarity. And we had some under Franklin Roosevelt, but look what happened. Once the Republican Party was able to win an election against the President of the United States [in 1944], that he took a back seat, a low back seat, and the orders were given by the Republican Party, and the Republican Party was, in other words, the FBI. The Federal Bureau of Investigation became the government of the United States, pushing out Franklin Roosevelt, who, while still President, was pushed out of that role, and his people were pushed out of that role.

And since that time, more or less, there has been no such thing as solidarity among American citizens. And therefore, we have to take the crises that we have to deal with, and we have to make sure that those crises actually mobilize us to a system of solidarity, real solidarity, where citizens are enabled to participate in what citizens and leaders of government at the same time, must deal with. And we don't have that. We haven't had that for a long, long time.

Question: I wonder if we all should remove our life savings, and close our accounts. Much is in 401Ks and life insurance policies. Those with regular savings, will they be affected? 401Ks? Insurance policies? I am prepared for chaos, no matter what comes. What do you think we should do?

We Don't Depend on Money

LaRouche: I think, first of all, you have to recognize what the nature of the problem is. Now, on the surface of what you're describing, I can understand that immediately; I don't have any problem with that. The problem is, what's the follow-up? What's the consequence of your trying to do something to deal with that problem, that misuse of economy? And that's where the problem lies.

You have to understand that what is being done to us now, is that through Wall Street and things like Wall Street in the United States in particular, what we're doing is we're jeopardizing the very existing life, personal life, of most people in the United States itself. And unless we interject action, to prevent that consequence from occurring....

We have to throw out President Obama, throw him out of office immediately; get rid of people in the government agencies, of government function, who do the same thing: who cheat; who steal and cheat. And yet they walk around day to day, place to place, and they are treated as authorities, authorities of the seats of government; or the members of Congress, and the institutions associated with those members of Congress. And these guys are committing murder, they're committing crimes against the people of the United States. The Wall Street gang should be cleaned out.

You have to go look at one thing: What did Franklin Roosevelt do when he became President? What did he do to deal with what had happened under Hoover and Hoover's associates? What did Franklin Roosevelt do? He was merciless. He put them in jail for great fraud. And he took the people who had been robbed,—all their access to wealth, even accumulation of savings and so forth, were being taken away from them: And Franklin Roosevelt intervened to deal with that. And what did he do? He acted to wipe out everything that was criminal about Wall Street and similar institutions. This is applied not only to the United States itself, but Franklin Roosevelt also understood that we had to deal with other nations, foreign nations on the same standard of judgment.

Now, we didn't always get our way on that thing from the United States, but we're in a time now, where you want to throw Wall Street out of existence, put 'em someplace where they beg, go beg, go beg for something. Because they've got nothing coming to them! They have robbed the people of the United States, they've cheated them to the bottom of everything.

Library of Congress

Rural electrification, one of FDR's major initiatives, in California's San Joaquin Valley in 1938.

What we need to do is mobilize the people, the citizens, to look at the problem,—look at the problem the way Franklin Roosevelt looked at this problem, the way he dealt with them. His action was correct. Now, what did he do? The United States was bankrupt; under Franklin Roosevelt, through the Hoover system the United States was bankrupt. How did Franklin Roosevelt save the United States from continuing to be bankrupt? By using the powers of government, the powers that lie in government, through the people, and to make sure that we provide credit, credit for people who have no employment but need it; who suffer from want.

What we did is, we changed the character of the United States, from Franklin Roosevelt's assumption of the Presidency to the point of the damned election of the Republicans which took the real power of Franklin Roosevelt out of his hands, and put it into the hands of really the same people within the Hoover circles.

And therefore, what we have to do is, we operate on the basis that the government of the United States will use its potential credit to assist in providing the opportunities of work and of necessity, as well, in order to build up the per-capita capabilities of the citizens within the United States, all kinds of citizens; and to do this by aid of making investments in creating construction. One of the greatest things was the so-called Hoover Dam, same thing.

So the idea is that we do not depend on counterfeit money; we do not depend upon money *per se*. We depend upon a system of credit, which has a valid base for advancing the productive powers of labor, of mankind in general. In other words, you take a person off the streets; they're absolutely hopeless in terms of their

New Yorkers pull down the statue of King George III on July 9, 1976.

loyalty to the British Crown, but in the last of the three documents, he is explicit in his demand that the colonies must submit to the "rule of law," i.e., they must obey the legal diktats of the British Crown and Parliament.

Hamilton wrote two replies to Seabury (A.W. Farmer), and it is in the second of those replies, titled "The Farmer Refuted," that the then eighteen-year-old Hamilton strikes directly at the foundation of oligarchical law. Written in February of 1775, two months prior to the battles of Lexington and Concord, "The Farmer Refuted" goes beyond Hamilton's first response to Seabury, wherein he had argued for the right of the newly formed Continental Congress to resist oppressive measures emanating from London; rather, in "The Farmer Refuted" Hamilton goes to the very heart of the matter at hand, i.e., the actual nature of law and government itself. Addressing "A.W. Farmer" directly, Hamilton says:

> There is so strong a similitude between your political principles and those maintained by Mr. [Thomas] Hobbes, that, in judging from them, a person might very easily mistake you for a disciple of his. His opinion was, exactly, coincident with yours, relative to man in a state of nature. He held, as you do, that he was, then, perfectly free from all restraint of law and government. Moral obligation, ac-

Law & Government: Hamilton vs. Hobbes

Jan. 3—Between late 1774 and early 1775 an exchange of five public letters took place between Alexander Hamilton and an individual who wrote under the pseudonym A.W. Farmer (A Westchester Farmer). At the time, A.W. Farmer's identity was unknown, but it was later revealed as Samuel Seabury, a prominent Anglican clergyman and a devoted loyalist to Britain during the American Revolution. Seabury later became the first American Episcopal bishop.

In three widely circulated public missives—"Free Thoughts on the Proceedings of the Continental Congress," "The Congress Canvassed," and "A View of the Controversy between Great Britain and her Colonies"—Seabury proclaimed not only his irrevocable

Continued on next page

financial situation. Franklin Roosevelt's administration gave provision to save people from dying on the streets! Like the streets of Manhattan!

And what we did is, we built up an economic growth inside the United States, within the term of Franklin Roosevelt prior to the new election, Wall Street elec-

tion. And we created the most powerful improvement in human life that mankind has ever experienced, heretofore. And that's the principle. We are responsible for the people; we who lead the nation, we are responsible for the care of the people. And when the care of the people is poor, because it's been stripped of its assets,

---

Law and Government: Hamilton vs. Hobbes
Continued from previous page

cording to him, is derived from the introduction of civil society; and there is no virtue, but what is purely artificial, the mere contrivance of politicians, for the maintenance of social intercourse. But the reason he ran into this absurd and impious doctrine, was, that he disbelieved the existence of an intelligent superintending principle, who is the governor, and will be the final judge of the universe.

Upon this law, depend the natural rights of mankind: the supreme being gave existence to man, together with the means of preserving and beatifying that existence. He endowed him with rational faculties, by the help of which, to discern and pursue such things, as were consistent with his duty and interest, and invested him with an inviolable right to personal liberty, and personal safety.

Hence, in a state of nature, no man had any moral power to deprive another of his life, limbs, property or liberty; nor the least authority to command, or exact obedience from him; except that which arose from the ties of consanguinity.

Hence also, the origin of all civil government, justly established, must be a voluntary compact, between the rulers and the ruled; and must be liable to such limitations, as are necessary for the security of the absolute rights of the latter; for what original title can any man or set of men have, to govern others, except their own consent? To usurp dominion over a people, in their own despite, or to grasp at a more extensive power than they are willing to entrust, is to violate that law of nature, which gives every man a right to his personal liberty; and can, therefore, confer no obligation to obedience.

When human laws contradict or discountenance the means, which are necessary to preserve the essential rights of any society, they defeat the proper end of all laws, and so become null and void.

Hamilton's reference to Thomas Hobbes is not capricious, for it was Hobbes, in his Leviathan (1651), who first enunciated the explicit doctrine of man-made Positive Law as supreme over human society, a theory of law divorced from any universal concept of morality or the human identity. So-called man-made "positive law" is grounded in the Thomas Hobbes/Adam Smith/Jeremy Bentham belief that human beings are beasts, motivated by the animalistic desire for the "pursuit of pleasure and avoidance of pain." The "rule of law," as defined by Hobbes, is a system of man-made law divorced from any higher concept of natural law, and it is to be imposed on the population through arbitrary rules, to which the people are required to submit.

In truth, this British concept of law, a notion of law designed to govern an oligarchical empire, was created in order to overturn and eradicate earlier Christian concepts of law, such as that of St. Thomas Aquinas, who asserted the primacy of natural law over man-made law, stating that where "it [man-made law] is at variance with natural law it will not be a law, but spoilt law."

Centuries later, in his *Letter from a Birmingham Jail* (1963), Dr. Martin Luther King would write:

A just law is a man-made code that squares with the moral law or the law of God. An unjust law is a code that is out of harmony with the moral law. To put it in the terms of St. Thomas Aquinas: An unjust law is a human law that is not rooted in eternal law and natural law.

---

it's the duty of government to promote the advancement of the skills and achievements of every citizen and every person. And that's our job.

What Is Our Government Now?

We do not depend upon other people's money! We depend upon what the United States represents in its characteristics of its institution, and we are determined to provide growth and advancement in the condition of life of the parts of the nation and the individuals of the nation. And that's what Franklin Roosevelt did! And that is the only thing that is worthwhile considering as a policy for planning for the condition of the United States right now, and for many other parts of the world also.

We just have to get back to that principle which Franklin Roosevelt, while in power, understood and demonstrated very clearly. We don't have to invent something new. We simply have to do what Franklin Roosevelt's Administration did, by putting Wall Street in jail, with serious jail time, among other things; and the loss of their money. And we've got to do the same thing again, which means, also, that the Federal government must act not to promote wealth as such, but to promote the growth of productivity of the citizens, and the results of that growth in terms of the benefits realized by human beings who are the citizens.

Question: My really big question is, does LaRouche PAC have Congressional support for the current effort? All I see thus far is, I can't see Congress taking action until after a big event of financial crisis or total executive misconduct. What do you think?

LaRouche: Well, he's right. The point is the present government, under the Bushes in particular, the Bush succession,—and Obama, is the worst of all possible Presidents to be considered so far. He's actually of a character of a Satanic characteristic. That is, his morality, or substitute for morality, is Satanic intrinsically. Every Tuesday, Obama has on the record so far,—has ordered people to be killed, with no valid protest of this, on this account. And they died; and Obama does that generally on Tuesdays. So you have a President who kills innocent citizens on his own impulses, and does it regularly.

White House/Pete Souza

President Obama announces one of his many murders—that of Osama bin Laden in May 2011.

Now you have a Congress, Congress in general; the Congress is fully aware of this! And what do they do about it? Nothing.

So what kind of a government do we have? We have a government. on the one hand, of professional Satanists; on the other hand, cowards. And that fact has to be rubbed in without remorse; rub it in!

You've got many members of Congress who are gutless wonders, and yet they call themselves the policymakers of nations. I don't think we need gutless wonders as members of Congress.

Question: Will the recent Seymour Hersh revelations of U.S. military giving Obama the middle finger and sharing intelligence with the Russians on the Daesh [ISIS], inspire Americans to take back their country?

LaRouche: I think I would read that a little bit differently. First of all, the entirety of the government of the United States today, pretty much all the officials and so forth, and especially Obama; Obama's among the worst mis-representatives of the United States: he's evil. Obama is an evil person. He should not have been President, ever! He's evil!

Now, the question of whether he's a President or not has come into doubt; of how Hillary lost the nomination for President to Obama. Now, that's a very strange thing, but in any case at a certain point I still thought that she was a valid person, and I spoke to her, and she asked my advice and I gave her my advice. But then she got under pressure from Obama. And from that standpoint on, things began to get pretty bad.

Now Hillary is not exactly a genius, not when it comes to science, nor when it comes to the profession of science; she never was. She was a lawyer, and she worked as a lawyer. And you have lawyers sometimes who are disenchanted by anything except the law profession.

The Legal Profession

Now, the law profession in the United States is filled with a lot of corruption. The courts are filled with corruption, because they treat legal matters, of law, they treat them in a certain way which is contrary to morality. They get by with doing things which a decent person would never allow to happen. And so, that's where the problem comes in: We don't really have checks and balances in any real sense, in terms of how the U.S. government is composed and how it is to operate,—we don't have it. Nor do we have it in our practice in general. The United States is dominated by Bertrand Russell's legacy, a kind of corruption, inherent corruption.

So the problem is, how can we get a system of government inside the United States which is fit for the use as the government of the United States? We have a few individuals who have a conscience in these matters, but those who have consciences have two problems, of two varieties: One variety is, they're very concerned; their conscience is stricken by what they did not do that they should have done. And the other is like Hillary, who doesn't give a damn what the truth is, when she's working for Obama, as she is now!

And she has no moral conscience in that sense. She may have a conscience for her daughter, a conscience for members of her family, this sort of thing; it's all personal stuff. But when it comes to the interaction among members of government, or bodies of government, these standards are corruption. And she's corrupt! She's inherently corrupt, morally corrupt! There's no doubt of it.

And so, there are a lot of people in the Congress and in the courts, who are corrupt in that way: They outnumber the people who are not corrupt, not necessarily in numbers, but in terms of influence. Some of the most powerful people in legislation, law generally, in government in general, are the worst, absolute worst, among the members of government of the United States.

That has to be changed, and it must be changed.

Frankly, It's Deadly—Cancel Dodd-Frank

by Rachel Brinkley

Jan. 1—The passage of Dodd-Frank 6 long years ago was a treasonous act against the United States and all humanity—unleashing evil effects which have not subsided, but multiplied, becoming a torrent of evil against the sacred rights of people everywhere. The imposition of this act represented President Obama's promise to maintain the systemic fraud in the financial system which has made possible the satanic pillaging of the American people at the hands of Wall-Street.

Worse, the "bail-in" bank account seizure provisions in Title II of the Dodd-Frank Act now threaten to unleash the greatest mass death through economic deprivation in human history—the very conditions which would guarantee the descent of civilization into thermonuclear World War III.

For this, each member of Congress who refuses to condemn the Dodd-Frank Act will be held accountable—that under the Nuremberg criteria of "known or should have known." Pleas of ignorance will not remove their responsibility for the effects of their decisions, especially those of the puppet author Barney Frank, if he can even be considered human.

As a candidate for Congress who ran against Barney Frank, I know more about his criminal behavior than he would probably like to remember about himself, but for now we need only focus on this one act—pushing mass-death against the people of the United States and world.

For example, since Barney and his Wall St. backers ushered in the bailout and trillions of dollars were poured down the drain with quantitative easing, death rates have skyrocketed. Since 2008, the numbers of homeless children have doubled, and heroin-related deaths have increased over 250%. The amount of Americans in poverty has grown from 37 to 47 million during Obama's presidency, food stamp recipients have grown from 28 million to 47 million, and one in five children are now living under the poverty line.

Meanwhile the global derivatives bubble has grown to $2 quadrillion dollars of worthless debt, endangering the entire world population as the collapse of the bubble will destroy the entire trans-Atlantic economic system and bring the world to nuclear war. The plummeting oil price is already hitting the fracking bubble, endangering oil investments, the junk bond market, and everything beyond.

Barnum Bailey fought to prevent the return of Glass-Steagall, which would have prevented this chaos and mass-murder, and intentionally forced through the designed-to-fail Frankly-Deadly Act, lying on behalf of Wall St., and against the will of the people. Yet, as Lyndon LaRouche forecast, these economic conditions are still but a faint foretaste of the economic implosion set for the beginning of this year, when the bail-in detonates in Europe and the United States (courtesy of the Frank-Dodd Act).

This can only be compared to the end of the Renaissance, as satanism took over the leadership of the churches in Europe, and the true notion of the higher, divine essence of mankind was crushed. Witness it today, as you see the current Pope acquiesce to the British Monarchy's satanic fraud of "man-made global warming"—a fraud designed for the purpose of contributing to the reduction of the world's population, and for crippling the general recognition of the creative powers of mankind.

Barney Frank is a criminal, he is damned evil and degenerate, and he should never have been allowed to hold congressional office. Yet, current members of Congress and presidential candidates are still using his advice to set the standard for law in this country! His authority should be completely cancelled! Congress must recognize that procedures of law must be held to a higher standard: that of natural law, which is not written by man.

Superficial congressmen may say: "See, we have made a choice, and put it on the books, and that therefore that is law." No, that is not true! In fact, mankind does not really make the law to which we all are subject. Law is the requirement of the human species to progress. If the human species is not progressing in its development and its fruition, then the law has been violated!

Dodd-Frank is treason and must be thrown out, to prevent the mass-murder and global war that will occur if nothing is done to change the current conditions. Franklin Roosevelt-style measures of emergency economic action, including Glass-Steagall, must be taken in the short term. Wall St. must be shut down! Obama must be thrown out, then we can throw their puppets Hillary, Trump, and Barney Frank into the sewer where they belong!

The United States Joins the New Silk Road: A Hamiltonian Vision For an Economic Renaissance

by Benjamin Deniston

In 2014 Helga Zepp-LaRouche commissioned the production of a road-map for expanding China's New Silk Road program into a fully global world land-bridge— The New Silk Road Becomes the World Land-Bridge. *In the winter of 2015 Mrs. Zepp-LaRouche called for the production of a shorter supplemental report focused on getting the United States on board with this program—* The United States Joins The New Silk Road: A Hamiltonian Vision For An Economic Renaissance.

The immediate future existence of the United States depends upon adopting this program now.

Jan. 3—There is an offer to the United States to join in a new orientation for the planet. China's New Silk Road program and its collaboration with the other BRICS nations in global development is creating a new paradigm on this planet, one of "win-win cooperation," and China has explicitly invited the United States to join in. Given

The World Land-Bridge

A view of plans for the World Land-Bridge from the perspective of the North Pole.

the current economic and cultural breakdown in the United States, this is a life-or-death opportunity for our nation.

The New Silk Road program is explicitly not a geopolitical move by China; it is not an attempt to defeat the United States. This is not an attempt by China, or China in cooperation with Russia, to control resources to the detriment of the United States, or to control regions of the planet to the detriment of the United States. This—as was stated repeatedly, explicitly by China—is based on a conception of "win-win" cooperation, premised on the understanding that the development of fundamental scientific and associated technological revolutions in cooperation with other nations, creates a net increase in the amount of wealth and resources available to the human species as a whole. We are at a point in mankind's development, such that if we do not rise to a level of international relations and global cooperation premised on that scientific understanding, we are not going to be able to exist as a civilization on this planet. If we continue the current mode of geopolitical conflict, we will destroy ourselves,—as Obama is threatening to do right now.

However, as Lyndon LaRouche presented in his December 28, 2015 discussion with the LaRouche PAC Policy Committee,[1] this alternative option is rooted in a higher form of natural law that society has to rise to meet. Mankind's fundamental nature is to progress, is to develop. You see a stark difference between China's orientation—the New Silk Road orientation, premised on this idea of win-win cooperation in large-scale development—versus what Pope Francis is now backing with his support of the "man-made climate change crisis" fraud—a British, Malthusian global population reduction program. The attempt to reduce carbon dioxide emissions typifies the genocidal, zero-growth imperial policy—a truly anti-human view—which must be eliminated.

Mankind has to progress. Creative progress is not just nice. It's not just good. *It is absolutely necessary for mankind to exist*. If we ever stop progressing, society degenerates, as the Twentieth Century trans-Atlantic civilization is now demonstrating. If you stop progressing, society destroys itself. But progress is not mathematical, not deductive. True progress is the type of unique, human, creative scientific advance typified by Kepler, typified by Einstein. This recognition of true

human creativity was attacked and for the most part destroyed by Bertrand Russell and his followers, on behalf of the British imperial system.

It is this understanding of human creativity as a unique principle in the universe that is the only *substance*; the *cause* of what enables mankind to act differently than animals, to fundamentally transform and improve his relationship to the universe. To, in effect, begin to separate himself from being just an Earth-based species; and be able to exist in the universe by mediating his existence through his creative relationship with the Solar System as a whole. That's a creative act that doesn't come from the fraudulent type of science that Bertrand Russell had attempted to impose; it comes from a unique form of human creative generation, unique acts of the human mind that do not come from sense perception, do not come from your empirical study of the world. But they come from human creativity *per se*, the understanding of truly human creative development, which has been attacked throughout the Twentieth Century.

That is the challenge we have to confront to save the United States. We can not simply attempt to reverse the degeneration that has occurred. We need a new fundamental law of human creative progress to become the guide-post for where mankind must go.

As Mr. LaRouche has stated, we are not just talking about changing some policy,—mankind's survival today depends upon a new Renaissance, a new creation of a higher understanding of mankind's nature and unique purpose and mission in the universe, as a creative force going into the Solar System. And going beyond the Solar System into the Galaxy, and understanding that it is something unique about the human mind and its creative potential that gives mankind the ability to do that. This is not just about reversing some bad policy; this is about developing a positive conception, a new discovery of what it is that enables mankind to progress, what it is that enables mankind to fulfill his true nature, what it is that makes mankind a unique force on this planet. A potential that no animal species exhibits.

If we don't understand that, if we do not premise the future on a new pursuit of those capabilities, mankind is not going to make it. Because that is what defines our existence; that is what defines the future. And if we don't rise to that level, as Mr. LaRouche has been warning, we are not going to make it through the current crisis.

---

1. In this issue.

The British Trigger Drive for Global War

by Jeffrey Steinberg

Jan. 5—The Jan. 2 mass executions by the Saudi regime, including the execution of the top Shi'ite cleric in the Kingdom, were not only an act of barbarism, in keeping with the Wahhabi/Salafi terrorism of the Islamic State. The action was aimed at triggering a new Hundred Years religious war within the Islamic world, pitting Sunni against Shia, and Arab against Persian.

Beyond the Greater Middle East region, the Saudi actions aim to fuel the ongoing war provocations against Russia and China, steered by President Barack Obama and British Prime Minister David Cameron on behalf of the British Crown, with the potential for a global thermonuclear war of annihilation.

To properly understand the full implications of the Saudi actions, some not-so-obvious factors must be taken fully into account, starting with the fact that the Saudi Monarchy is a pawn of the British Empire, and has been so from its founding. Under the current rule of King Salman, the most extreme form of Wahhabi fundamentalism has been brought to the fore, and this is perfectly in keeping with the British agenda of permanent population warfare.

The most critical factor, however, is the onrushing collapse of the global British System, which dominates the financial and monetary policies of the entire trans-Atlantic region. Not only is that system crashing at an accelerating rate, as events since the start of the New Year have evidenced. The

epicenter of the disintegration is the trans-Atlantic region itself, including the United States, Britain, and continental Europe,—while the Asia-Pacific region, led by a growing collaboration between China, Russia, and India, is relatively prospering and growing. While the disintegration of the trans-Atlantic region will clearly impact on the Asia-Pacific theater, the collaborative projects there, including China's "One Belt, One Road" program, and its intersection with Russia's Eurasian Economic Union program, will buffer Eurasia against the most immediate shocks of the collapse.

It is because of this emerging China-Russia-India collaboration that London is intent on provoking war

EIRNS/Alicia Cerretani

Congressman Walter Jones (R-NC), the lead sponsor of the House bill calling for the release of the 28 pages of Congressional Joint Inquiry Report on 9/11, at one of the many press conferences he's held to promote the bill. He is joined here by family members of victims.

with both Moscow and Beijing—and using the remaining months of the Obama presidency to pull it off.

Both the European Union and the United States have instituted bail-in programs, in effect as of Jan. 1, 2016 throughout Europe (and already in place in the United States since the passage of the 2010 Dodd-Frank Act, under which bank deposits can be stolen as part of a desperate and futile effort to save the bankrupt too-big-to-fail financial institutions). Those too-big-to-fail financial institutions have amassed a derivatives exposure well above $1 quadrillion, and a $5 trillion junk-bond and bank debt bubble, tied to the shale oil and gas sector, is immediately set to detonate.

The bail-in swindle is not only a recipe for mass social chaos, but is a measure of just how desperate the defenders of the British System are at this moment. They are desperate enough to go for global confrontation with Russia and China, rather than surrender their power.

This is the context for understanding why the Saudi butchers were encouraged to carry out the mass executions, knowing it would set off a process of conflict and chaos throughout the Persian Gulf and Southwest Asia.

Release the 28 Pages

The Saudi barbarism cannot go unanswered. The most efficient action, already in front of the United States Congress and the Obama Administration, is to release the 28-page chapter from the original Joint Congressional Inquiry into 9/11, which documented the Saudi Monarchy's hand behind the Sept. 11, 2001 attacks on the World Trade Center and the Pentagon.

The central figure in the Saudi promotion of the 9/11 attacks was Prince Bandar bin-Sultan, a son of the late Defense Minister and Crown Prince, Sultan bin Abdulaziz. Prince Bandar was Saudi Ambassador to the United States for decades, up through the 9/11 attacks. He bankrolled at least two of the lead hijackers, and was also the bridge between Britain and Saudi Arabia in the infamous al-Yamamah barter deal, which bound London and Riyadh together in managing the biggest offshore covert funds for running terrorism. The al-Yamamah deal, first consummated in 1985 by Bandar and then-British Prime Minister Margaret Thatcher, continues to the present, and has been the source of

kremlin.ru

Russian President Vladimir Putin giving his New Year's address.

funding for almost every jihadist terrorist front, dating from the original Arab-Afghan Legions that spawned al-Qaeda and the Islamic State.

Russians Address Reality

Russian President Vladimir Putin, along with his Chinese counterpart, President Xi Jinping, is fully aware of the war provocations directed against Russia and China, and Russia has made major strides in the past several years to beef up its military capacities in response.

On New Year's Eve, President Putin signed a new Russian National Security Strategy, the first such broad policy statement since 2009. The document made the point that, while Russia seeks cooperation and equal partnership with the United States and NATO, the actions taken by Western powers, including the violent coup d'état in Ukraine in 2014, are seen as a serious national security threat to Russia. The document detailed the threats coming from jihadist terrorists, and from non-governmental organizations and state agencies promoting regime change, ultimately targeting Russia itself.

The document also emphasized that a major source of global instability was the crisis in the world financial system, stating that "Against the background of structural imbalances in the global economy and the financial system, the growth of sovereign debt, and energy market volatility, the risk of a repeated major financial and economic crisis remains high."

Soon after the document's release and circulation, the Chinese government announced its endorsement of the paper, and vowed to expand Russian-Chinese strategic partnership collaboration.

American Voices Warn of World War Threat

The direct policy warnings coming out of Moscow have reverberated in the United States as well, with some leading voices warning about the danger of thermonuclear world war, which stems from the Obama Administration's continuing commitment to regime change against the Bashar al-Assad government in Syria. Rep. Tulsi Gabbard (D-Ha.) has been the leading spokesperson for those within the military-intelligence establishment (she served two terms in combat in Iraq) who demand that Obama drop the regime-change schemes, because they can lead to direct confrontation with Russia. Rep. Gabbard has introduced a bill into the House of Representatives, barring the United States from seeking the overthrow of the Assad government.

Former Clinton Administration Secretary of Defense William Perry has also come out sharply, warning about the danger of nuclear war, stemming from the U.S. policy of confrontation with Russia. Perry has published a new memoir, *My Journey at the Nuclear Brink*, which not only recounts his own experiences in fighting to avoid a nuclear confrontation, but warns that the danger of nuclear war is greater today than during the height of the Cold War. In a recent interview with Sputnik News, Perry was blunt: "I see an imperative to stop this damn nuclear race before it gets under way again, not just for the cost, but for the danger it puts all of us in."

In a quasi-official statement of warning along the same lines, the U.S. Army's most prestigious journal, *Military Review*, published a series of three article in the latest edition, clearly stating the actual Russian military doctrine and calling for the United States to develop a cooperative approach to Moscow. The first two articles were reprints of President Putin's address to the United Nations General Assembly in Sept. 2015, and the Feb. 2013 address by Chief of the Russian General Staff, Gen. Valery Gerasimov, to the Academy of Military Sciences.

The third article, by Charles K. Bartles, a Russia specialist at the Army's Foreign Military Studies Office at Fort Leavenworth, explained the actual Russian military policy, in response to the new NATO-USA doctrine of color revolutions and regime change. Echoing earlier warnings by Anthony Cordesman of the Center for Strategic and International Studies (CSIS), Bartles emphasized that it is imperative for Western strategists to understand and appreciate the Russian assessments and policies, and not to buy the hokey Western propaganda that it is Russia that has adopted the policy of hybrid asymmetric warfare.

Despite these voices of warning, the greatest danger today stems from the fact that too few people in the know are willing to act before it is too late. Congress fled town at the end of 2015 without addressing the imminent blowout of the financial system, and loud voices in Congress and among a majority of presidential candidates are pressing the very policies that can lead to a war of annihilation.

The mere fact that President Obama remains in office, after having violated the Constitution repeatedly, is a testament to the bankruptcy of official Washington. Going into 2016, the consequences of failing to reverse course can and will be catastrophic.

Unsurvivable

A dark, gruesome, but wholly true depiction of the threat of thermonuclear war, its consequences, and Obama's deployment of a major portion of the U.S. thermonuclear capabilities in multiple theaters threatening both Russia and China.

http://larouchepac.com/unsurvivable